Pocket R...

...IAP

Written and researched by

JONATHAN BUCKLEY

Contents

<< GONDOLAS AND VIEW OF SAN GIORGIO MAGGIORE
< GONDALIERS IN CANNAREGIO'S CANALS

3

INTRODUCTION TO

VENICE

Founded 1500 years ago on a cluster of mudflats in the centre of the lagoon, Venice rose to become Europe's main trading post between the West and the East, and at its height controlled an empire that extended from the Dolomites to Cyprus. The fabric of the present-day city, astonishingly well preserved, bears testimony to Venice's former grandeur in virtually every square and street.

THE CAMPANILE, SAN MARCO

Best place for a picnic

The beauty of the cityscape and the price of restaurants make picnicking an enticing proposition in Venice – but there are strict by-laws against picnics in the city squares. So buy provisions at Rialto market then hop on a vaporetto to Giardini, where you'll find shade, a bit of greenery, and a fabulous panorama of Venice and the lagoon.

See Giardini > p.114

In the heyday of the Venetian Republic, some two hundred thousand people lived in Venice, three times its present population. Merchants from Europe and western Asia maintained warehouses here; transactions in the banks and bazaars of the Rialto dictated the value of commodities all over the continent; in the dockyards of the Arsenale the workforce was so vast that a warship could be built and fitted out in a single day; and the Piazza San Marco was thronged with people here to set up deals or report to the Republic's government. Nowadays it's no longer a buzzing metropolis but rather the embodiment of a fabulous past, dependent for its survival largely on the people who come to marvel at its relics.

The monuments that draw the largest crowds are the Basilica di San Marco – the mausoleum of the city's patron saint – and the Palazzo Ducale or Doge's Palace. Certainly these are the most imposing structures in the city, but a roll-call of the churches worth visiting would feature more than a dozen names. Many of

When to visit

Venice's tourist season is very nearly an all-year affair. Peak season, when hotel rooms are difficult to come by at short notice, is from **April to October**; try to avoid **July and August**, when the climate becomes oppressively hot and clammy. The other two popular spells are the **Carnevale** (leading up to Lent) and the weeks on each side of **Christmas**.

For the ideal combination of comparative peace and a mild climate, the two or three weeks **immediately preceding Easter** are perhaps best. **November and December** are somewhat less reliable: some days bring fogs that make it difficult to see from one bank of the Canal Grande to the other. If you want to see the city at its quietest, **January** is the month to go – take plenty of warm clothes, though, as the winds off the Adriatic can be savage, and you should be prepared for floods throughout the winter. This **acqua alta**, as Venice's seasonal flooding is called, has been an element of Venetian life for centuries, but nowadays it's far more frequent than it used to be: between October and late February it's not uncommon for flooding to occur several days in succession.

the city's treasures remain in the churches for which they were created, but a sizeable number have been removed to one or other of Venice's museums, with the Accademia holding the lion's share. This cultural heritage is a source of endless fascination, but you should also discard your itineraries for a day and just wander – the anonymous parts of Venice reveal as much of the city as its well-known attractions.

The historic centre of Venice is made up of 118 islands, tied together by some four hundred bridges to form an amalgamation that's divided into six large administrative districts known as *sestieri*, three on each side of the Canal Grande.

TRAGHETTO ON THE CANAL GRANDE

VENICE AT A GLANCE

>>EATING AND DRINKING

Near the Piazza the quality of restaurants is generally poor and prices inflated. However, out in the quieter zones Venice has an increasing number of excellent **restaurants**, in which fresh fish and seafood predominate. The three best areas to head for are **Dorsoduro** (San Barnaba and Campo Santa Margherita), the **Rialto district** and northern **Cannaregio**.

One of the most appealing aspects of Venetian social life is encapsulated in the phrase *"andemo a ombra"*, literally an invitation to go into the shade, but in fact an invitation for a drink – more specifically, a small glass of wine (an *ombra*); an **enoteca** is a bar specializing in wines. Also distinctively Venetian is the **bácaro**, a **bar** that offers a range of snacks called **cicheti** (or *cicheti*); usually €1–2.50 per portion, they may include *polpette* (small beef and garlic meatballs), *carciofini* (artichoke hearts) and *polipi* (baby octopus or squid). Many *bácari* also produce one or two main dishes, such as risotto or seafood pasta. Excellent food is also served at many **osterie**, the simplest of which have just three or four tables, while others have sizeable dining areas. And to further blur the division between places to eat and drink, Venice's restaurants often have a separate street-side bar. Venetians tend to eat early: don't turn up after 8.30pm.

>>NIGHTLIFE

Venice is notorious for its lack of **nightlife**, though it does have a good number of late-opening bars, some of which have live music or DJs, though the venues tend to be small and there are strict by-laws against late-night noise. The best of these are in Dorsoduro, where the university is based, and the Rialto has also livened up recently. Music in Venice, to all intents and purposes, means classical music – though the Teatro Malibran does stage concerts by Italian rock bands from time to time. The top-bracket **music venues** are La Fenice, the Teatro Malibran and the Teatro Goldoni, all in the San Marco *sestiere*.

>>SHOPPING

The main retail zones in Venice are the **Mercerie** (immediately north of Piazza San Marco) and **Calle Larga XXII Marzo** (west of the Piazza). Nowadays, they are dominated by famous Italian brands such as Gucci, Prada and Trussardi. In quieter parts of the city, notably in San Polo, some authentically Venetian outlets and workshops are still in operation. The manufacture of exquisite decorative papers is a distinctively Venetian skill; small craft studios in various parts of the city continue to produce beautiful handmade bags and shoes; and of course there are lots of shops selling glass, lace and Carnival masks – the quintessential souvenir.

OUR RECOMMENDATIONS FOR WHERE TO EAT, DRINK AND SHOP ARE LISTED AT THE END OF EACH PLACES CHAPTER.

Day One in Venice

1 **Basilica di San Marco** > p.34.
Begin at the heart of the city, the
Piazza San Marco and the Basilica –
and get here early, before the queues
for the cathedral build up.

Pause for coffee > p.48.
Rosa Salva is an excellent
option, not far from the Piazza.

2 **Palazzo Ducale** > p.36. Explore
the Doge's Palace, a vast and
fascinating building, which will take
up most of the rest of the morning.

Lunch > Ramble west,
away from the Piazza itself,
to *Al Bacareto* (see p.56), which has
been going for decades, and is always
dependable.

3 **Santo Stefano and Santa
Maria del Giglio** > p.52 & p.51. Loop
back towards the Piazza, dropping in
at these two churches, and maybe
window-shopping on Calle Larga XXII
Marzo, the most upmarket street in
the city.

4 **Correr museum, Libreria
and archeological museum** > p.40.
The rambling Correr museum gives you
some essential historical background
– and it has a fine art gallery and
archeological museum.

Evening in the Rialto >
From the Piazza, saunter
along the shopping streets of the
Mercerie (see p.44), as a prelude
to crossing the Rialto Bridge for an
aperitivo and dinner in the market
district (see p.74), where you'll find
some atmospheric local bars.

Day Two in Venice

1 The Accademia > p.58. The city's main art gallery – one of Europe's great collections – and worth several hours of your time.

2 Salute and the Záttere > p.62 & 63. Visit the great church of the Salute, en route to the Záttere, where the views are fantastic.

3 San Trovaso > p.64. Strike north from Záttere, and look in on the oldest remaining gondola workshop in the city.

 Lunch > Head to Campo di Santa Margherita (see p.66), a buzzing square where you can revive yourself at one of its many bars and cafés.

4 The Frari > p.82. Continue north from Campo di Santa Margherita to the city's mightiest Gothic church, which features a couple of first-rate works by Titian.

5 Scuola Grande di San Rocco > p.83. The Scuola features a stupendous cycle of Tintoretto paintings.

6 San Zanipolo > p.100. Stroll to Piazzale Roma, then take the #5.2 vaporetto to Fondamente Nove, which is close to the city's other gargantuan church, San Zanipolo (Santi Giovanni e Paolo).

Evening in Cannaregio > p.88. From Zanipolo you can wander westward into Cannaregio; the bars and restaurants of northern Cannaregio are among the best in Venice – *Anice Stellato* (see p.98) is a particular favourite.

Off the beaten track

To get a feel for genuine Venice, you'll need to explore the peripheries of the city, where you'll find some atmospheric quarters and intriguing sights.

1 San Sebastiano and Angelo Raffaele > p.65 & p.66. These neighbouring churches make a great start to a day in Venice's less touristed zones.

2 San Nicolò dei Mendicoli > p.66. Now walk to the western edge of Dorsoduro and the ancient church of San Nicolò dei Mendicoli.

3 Tolentini > p.85. Stroll along the canal north from here and you'll be heading in the right direction for the Tolentini church; the Giardino Padadopoli is also close at hand, and a good spot for a sit down.

Lunch > In front of the Tolentini you'll find *Da Lele* (see p.87), a terrific spot for a sandwich and glass of inexpensive wine.

4 The Ghetto > p.90. From nearby Piazzale Roma, the #4.2 and #5.2 will take you to Guglie, the nearest stop to the Ghetto.

5 Madonna dell'Orto > p.92. A short way north of the Ghetto, you'll find Tintoretto's parish church, one of the most beautiful in Venice.

6 San Pietro > p.113. From the Madonna dell'Orto stop, take the #5.2 all the way to San Pietro, where the city's former cathedral nestles amid boatyards.

Dinner in eastern Castello. The #5.2 continues over to the Lido, then bounces back, via Sant'Elena, to Giardini. For dinner you could choose between two of the very best restaurants in the city: *Corte Sconta* or *Al Covo* (see p.115).

On the water

One long boat-trip is absolutely essential for any visit to Venice. Arm yourself with a travel pass, and head out to some of the further-flung islands.

1 Torcello > p.128. The hour-long voyage out to the island of Torcello, where the settlement of the lagoon began, is a treat in itself, and the ancient cathedral is a magnificent thing.

2 Burano > p.128. On your way back, get off at the lace-making island of Burano for an hour or so.

3 Murano > p.127. And then jump back on board for Murano and its glass factories.

 Lunch > Eat at Murano's ever-excellent *Busa alla Torre* (p.131).

4 San Zaccaria > p.106. From Murano the #4.2 goes all the way to San Zaccaria – its waterlogged crypt brings home just how perilous the city's relationship with the water is.

5 The Arsenale > p.112. Take a look at the former powerhouse of the Venetian economy.

6 San Giorgio Maggiore > p.132. Take the #2 over to San Giorgio Maggiore, not just for its architecture and paintings, but for the superb panorama from the top of its campanile.

7 La Giudecca > p.134. Hop back on the #2 for one stop to reach La Giudecca. There's one great building here – the Redentore – but most of the island is a residential district, with boatyards along its southern shore.

8 The Canal Grande by night > p.152. End the day with a night-time voyage down the city's main thoroughfare, on the unhurried #1 or #N vaporetto.

Big sights

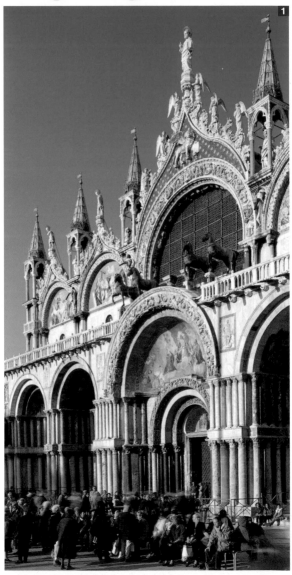

1 The Basilica di San Marco The mosaic-encrusted church of St Mark is the most opulent cathedral in all of Europe.**> p.34**

2 The Accademia In the Accademia's magnificent galleries you can trace the development of painting in Venice from the fifteenth century to the eighteenth, the last golden age of Venetian art. > **p.58**

4 The Frari The gargantuan edifice of Santa Maria Gloriosa dei Frari contains masterpieces by Titian, Bellini, Donatello and many more. > **p.82**

3 The Scuola Grande di San Rocco Rome has the Sistine Chapel, Florence has the Brancacci Chapel, and Venice has the Scuola Grande di San Rocco, with its overwhelming cycle of paintings by Jacopo Tintoretto. > **p.83**

5 The Palazzo Ducale The home of the doges was the nerve-centre of the entire Venetian empire, and was decorated by some of the greatest Venetian artists. > **p.36**

The main islands

1 Burano The brightly painted exteriors of the houses of Burano give this island an appearance that's distinct from any other settlement in the lagoon.
> p.128

2 La Giudecca Once one of the city's main industrial zones, La Giudecca is nowadays a predominantly residential area that retains much of the spirit of the city prior to the age of mass tourism. > **p.134**

3 San Michele Located a short distance north of the city centre, San Michele is possibly the most beautiful cemetery in the world. > **p.124**

4 Torcello The majestic cathedral of Torcello – the oldest building in the whole lagoon – marks the spot where the lagoon city came into existence. > **p.128**

5 Murano Glass has been the basis of Murano's economy for seven hundred years, and there are still plenty of factories where you can admire the glassblowers' amazing skills. > **p.127**

Museums and galleries

1 **Ca' d'Oro** Once the most extravagant house on the Canal Grande, the Ca' d'Oro today is home to an engagingly miscellaneous art collection. > **p.94**

2 The Guggenheim For a break from the Renaissance, spend an hour or two with the Guggenheim's fine array of modern art. **> p.60**

3 Ca' Rezzonico Devoted to the visual and applied arts of the eighteenth century, the Ca' Rezzonico contains several wonderful paintings and some frankly bizarre furniture.**> p.68**

4 Museo Correr Now joined to the Libreria Sansoviniana and the archeological museum, the Correr is a museum of Venetian history with an excellent art gallery upstairs **> p.40**

5 Punta della Dogana The Pinault Collection is a stunner – installed in the dazzlingly revamped customs house, this is Europe's largest display of contemporary art. **> p.61**

Venice viewpoints

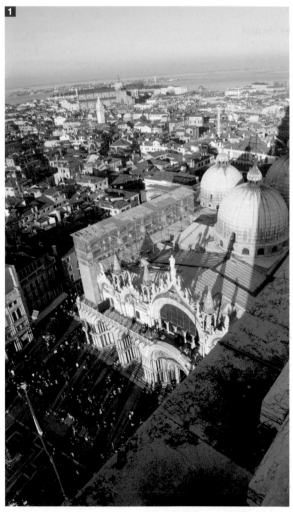

1 Campanile di San Marco The cathedral's belltower – the tallest structure for miles around – affords grandstand views of the historic centre.
> p.38

2 The Riva
Stretching from the Palazzo Ducale to the Arsenale, the Riva degli Schiavoni is Venice's finest promenade – an unforgettable experience at sunset. **> p.106**

3 The boat to Burano For a long-range perspective on the whole of the city, take a trip on the #12 vaporetto from Fondamente Nove out to Burano. **> p.124**

4 San Giorgio Maggiore The one thing you can't see from the Campanile di San Marco is the Campanile di San Marco, which is one reason why the best of all lookouts is the belltower of San Giorgio Maggiore, across the water. **> p.132**

5 The Záttere The southern waterfront of Dorsoduro, formerly a busy dock, is nowadays a perfect place for an unhurried stroll and café-stop. **> p.63**

Restaurants

1 Alla Fontana The tiny, homely *Alla Fontana* offers superb traditional seafood at very reasonable prices. **> p.98**

2 La Bitta If you feel you can't look another squid in the face, try *La Bitta*, a terrific small *osteria* where meat rules the menu. **> p.72**

3 Corte Sconta Imaginative cuisine and a friendly atmosphere have made *Corte Sconta* a huge success – reservations are almost obligatory. **> p.115**

4 Anice Stellato The modern styling and consistently high standards of *Anice Stellato* have made it one of the new stars of the Venice restaurant scene. **> p.98**

5 Osteria di Santa Marina If you ask any Venetian to name the top five restaurants in Venice, the refined *Osteria di Santa Marina* is sure to be on the list. **> p.109**

Renaissance art and architecture

1 San Zaccaria A large and lustrous altarpiece by Giovanni Bellini is the highlight inside this wonderful building. **> p.106**

3 The Libreria Sansoviniana and the Zecca Standing side by side opposite the Palazzo Ducale, the city library and mint were both created by Jacopo Sansovino, the Republic's principal architect in the early sixteenth century. > **p.42**

2 San Michele in Isola Designed by Mauro Codussi, this beguiling little church was one of the first Renaissance buildings in Venice. > **p.124**

4 San Sebastiano The parish church of Paolo Veronese is a treasure-house of pictures by the artist, begun before he had turned 30. > **p.65**

5 San Giorgio Maggiore Palladio's famed church of San Giorgio Maggiore is home to a pair of paintings that Tintoretto created specifically for the place where they still hang. > **p.132**

Bars

1 **Al Volto** The Veneto produces more DOC (Denominazione di origine controllata) wines than any other region of Italy, and there's nowhere better to sample them than *Al Volto*. **> p.49**

2 Cantina del Vino già Schiavi Known locally as *Al Bottegon*, the *Cantina del Vino* is one of Venice's best old-style *bácari* (wine and snack bars). **> p.73**

3 Do Mori
No seats, no tables – just good wine and good snacks. *Do Mori* is one of the last of a dying breed. **> p.87**

4 Café Noir Open till the small hours, *Café Noir* is a fixture of the student social scene. **> p.72**

5 Enoteca Mascareta You really can't go home without having first tried *cartizze*, the finest type of prosecco; drop into *Mascareta* to sample a glass of it. **> p.109**

Cafés, cakes and ice cream

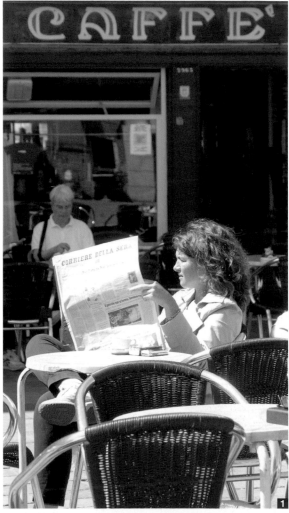

1 Il Caffè If the Piazza now belongs to the tourists, Campo di Santa Margherita belongs firmly to the Venetians – soak up the atmosphere at the place known locally as *Caffè Rosso*. > **p.71**

2 Florian The most famous café in all of Italy – just try not to keel over when they give you the bill. **> p.43**

3 Nico Take a slab of praline ice cream, slather it with cream, and you've got a *gianduiotto da passeggio*, the speciality at *Nico*. **> p.71**

4 Rosa Salva It doesn't have the glamour of *Florian*, but *Rosa Salva's* coffee is every bit as good. The Zanipolo branch is the best. **> p.108**

5 Caffè del Doge This bright and smart Rialto café is run by a company that's been supplying the city with superb coffee for more than sixty years. **> p.86**

29

San Marco: the Piazza

The *sestiere* of San Marco – a rectangle smaller than 1000m by 500m – has been the nucleus of Venice from the start of the city's existence. The Piazza San Marco was where the first rulers built their citadel – the Palazzo Ducale – and it was here that they established their most important church – the Basilica di San Marco. Over the succeeding centuries the Basilica evolved into the most ostentatiously rich church in Christendom, and the Palazzo Ducale grew to accommodate and celebrate Venice's system of government. Meanwhile, the setting for these two great edifices developed into a public space so dignified that no other square in the city was thought fit to bear the name "piazza" – all other Venetian squares are campi or campielli. Nowadays the San Marco area is home to the city's plushest hotels, while elegant and exorbitant cafés spill out onto the pavement from the Piazza's arcades, and the swankiest shops in Venice line the streets that radiate from it.

The government of Venice

Virtually from the beginning, the **government of Venice** was dominated by the merchant class, who in 1297 enacted a measure known as the **Serrata del Maggior Consiglio** (Closure of the Great Council). From then onwards, any man not belonging to one of the wealthy families on the list compiled for the *Serrata* was ineligible to participate in the running of the city. After a while, this list was succeeded by a register of patrician births and marriages called the **Libro d'Oro**, upon which all claims to membership of the elite were based. By the second decade of the fourteenth century, the constitution of Venice had reached a form that was to endure until the coming of Napoleon; its civil and criminal code, defined in the early thirteenth century, was equally resistant to change.

What made the political system stable was its web of counterbalancing councils and committees, and its exclusion of any youngsters. Most patricians entered the Maggior Consiglio at 25 and could not expect a middle-ranking post before 45; from the middle ranks to the top was another long haul – the average age of the doge from 1400 to 1600 was 72.

The **doge** was the figurehead of the Republic rather than anything akin to its president, and numerous restrictions were placed on his activities – all his letters were read by censors, for example. On the other hand, whereas his colleagues on the various state councils were elected for terms as brief as a month, the doge was **elected for life** and sat on all the major councils, which at the very least made him extremely influential.

Piazza San Marco

Rio dei Ferali

CAMPO SAN GIOVANNI NOVO

C. DEI PRETI

RIO TERRA DELLE COLONNE

C. DEGLI SPECCHIER

CALLE SPADARIA

MERCERIA DELL'OROLOGIO

CALLE DEGLI ANGELO

SAN MARCO

CALLE LARGA

C. DELLA CANONICA

Palazzo Trevisan

CAMPO SANTI FILIPPO E GIACOMO

CALLE FIUBERA

CALLE DEI FABBRI

❶ Palazzo Patriarcale

Torre dell' Orologio

San Basso

PIAZZETTA DEI LEONCINI

Museo Diocesano

Rio di Palazzo

CALLE DEGLI ALBANESI

C. DEL CAVALLETTO

Rio del Cavalletto

❷

Basilica di San Marco

Bacino Orseolo

Procuratie Vecchie

Campanile

PIAZZA SAN MARCO

Porta della Carta

Ponte dei Sospiri

C. SCOLASTICA

Palazzo Prigioni

RIVA DEGLI SCHIAVONI

CALLE LARGA DELL'ASCENSIONE

Ala Napoleonica

Libreria Sansoviniana

PIAZZETTA SAN MARCO

Palazzo Ducale

Ponte della Paglia

❸ Procuratie Nuove (Museo Correr)

Museo Archeologico

MOLO SAN MARCO

CALLE VALLARESSO

Rio dei Giardinetti

Giardinetti Reali

Zecca

FOND. DEI GIARDINETTI AC/ACL

Bacino di San Marco

ⓘ

N

0 metres 100
0 yards 100

SAN MARCO 1-2-N

SHOPS	
Martinuzzi	3
Seguso	2
Venini	1

CAFÉS AND PASTICCERIE	
Florian	3
Lavena	1
Quadri	2

THE BASILICA DI SAN MARCO

Mon–Sat 9.45am–4.45pm, Sun 2–5pm; the Loggia dei Cavalli is open Sun am. Free for main part of church, but admission fees totalling €10.50 are charged for certain areas. Large bags must be left, free of charge, at nearby Calle San Basso 315a. MAP P.33, POCKET MAP G14–H14

All over Venice you see images of the lion of St Mark holding a book on which is carved the text "Pax tibi, Marce evangelista meus. Hic requiescet corpus tuum" ("Peace be with you Mark, my Evangelist. Here shall your body rest"). These supposedly are the words with which St Mark was greeted by an angel who appeared to him on the night he took shelter in the lagoon on his way back to Rome. Having thus assured themselves of the sacred ordination of their city, the first Venetians duly went about fulfilling the angelic prophecy. In 828 two merchants stole the body of St Mark from its tomb in Alexandria and brought it back to Venice. Work began immediately on a shrine to house him, and the Basilica di San Marco was consecrated in 832. The amazing church you see today is essentially the version built in 1063–94, embellished in the succeeding centuries.

THE EXTERIOR

The marble-clad exterior is adorned with numerous pieces of ancient stonework, but a couple of features warrant special attention: the **Romanesque carvings** of the arches of the central doorway; and the group of porphyry figures set into the wall on the waterfront side – known as the **Tetrarchs**, in all likelihood they're a fourth-century Egyptian work depicting Diocletian and his three co-rulers of the unravelling Roman Empire. The real **horses of San Marco** are inside the church – the four outside are modern replicas. On the main facade, the only ancient mosaic to survive is *The Arrival of the Body of St Mark*, above the **Porta di Sant'Alipio** (far left); made around 1260, it features the earliest known image of the Basilica.

Just inside, the intricately patterned stonework of the **narthex floor** is mostly eleventh- and twelfth-century,

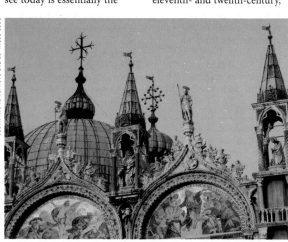
ROOF DETAIL OF THE BASILICA DI SAN MARCO

INTERIOR OF THE BASILICA DI SAN MARCO

while the majority of the **mosaics** on the domes and arches constitute a series of Old Testament scenes dating from the thirteenth century.

On the right of the main door from the narthex into the body of the church is a steep staircase up to the **Museo Marciano** and the **Loggia dei Cavalli** (daily 9.45am–4.45pm; €5), home of the fabled horses. Thieved from Constantinople in 1204, the horses are almost certainly Roman works of the second century, and are the only *quadriga* (group of four horses harnessed to a chariot) to have survived from the classical world. The scratches and the partial gilding on the horses' skin are original, added in order to catch the sunlight.

THE INTERIOR

With its undulating floor of patterned marble and 4000 square metres of mosaics, the interior of the Basilica is the most opulent of any cathedral in Europe. Officially the remains of St Mark lie in the sarcophagus underneath the high altar, at the back of which you can see the most precious of San Marco's treasures, the astonishing **Pala d'Oro** (€2.50) – the "golden altar screen". Commissioned in 976 in Constantinople, the *Pala* was enlarged, enriched and rearranged by Byzantine goldsmiths in 1105, then by Venetians in 1209 to incorporate some of the less cumbersome loot from the Fourth Crusade, and again (finally) in 1345. Tucked into the corner of the south transept is the door of the **treasury** (€3), which includes an unsurpassed collection of Byzantine silver and gold work.

Another marvel is the **rood screen**, surmounted by marble figures of The Virgin, St Mark and the Apostles (1394) by Jacobello and Pietro Paolo Dalle Masegne. Finally, Venice's most revered religious image, the tenth-century **Icon of the Madonna of Nicopeia**, stands in the chapel on the east side of the north transept; until 1204 it was one of the most revered icons in Constantinople, where it used to be carried ceremonially at the head of the emperor's army.

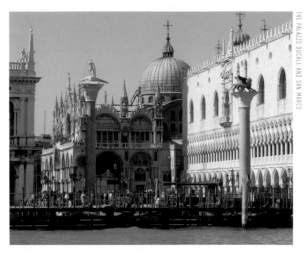

THE PALAZZO DUCALE

Ⓦ palazzoducale.visitmuve.it. Daily:
April–Oct 8.30am–7pm; Nov–March
8.30am–5.30pm. Entrance only with Museum
Pass or San Marco museums card. MAP P.33,
POCKET MAP G14–H14

Architecturally, the Palazzo
Ducale is a unique mixture:
the style of its exterior, with its
geometrically patterned
stonework and continuous
tracery walls, can only be called
Islamicized Gothic, whereas the
courtyards and much of the
interior are based on Classical
forms – a blending of
influences that led Ruskin to
declare it "the central building
of the world". Unquestionably,
it is the finest secular building
of its era in Europe, and the
central building of Venice: it
was the residence of the doge,
the home of all of Venice's
governing councils, its law
courts, a sizeable number of its
civil servants and even its
prisons. All power in the
Venetian Republic was
controlled within this building.

The original doge's fortress
was founded at the start of the
ninth century, but it was in the
fourteenth and fifteenth

centuries that the Palazzo
Ducale acquired its present
shape. The principal entrance,
the **Porta della Carta**, was
commissioned in 1438 by Doge
Francesco Fóscari, and is one
of the most ornate Gothic
works in the city. The
passageway into the Palazzo
ends under the **Arco Fóscari**,
which you can see only after
getting your ticket, as visitors
are nowadays directed in
through the arcades on the
lagoon side.

From the ticket office you're
directed straight into the
Museo dell'Opera, where the
originals of most of the superb
capitals from the external
loggias are well displayed. From
ground level you are directed
up the Scala dei Censori to the
upper arcade and then up the
gilded **Scala d'Oro**, the main
internal staircase of the Palazzo
Ducale.

THE STATE ROOMS

A subsidiary staircase leads
to the **Doge's Apartments**
(look out for Titian's small
fresco of *St Christopher*), then
the Scala d'Oro continues up

to the *secondo piano nobile*, where you soon enter the **Anticollegio**. With its pictures by Tintoretto and Veronese, this is one of the richest rooms in the Palazzo Ducale, and no doubt made a suitable impact on the emissaries who waited here for admission to the **Sala del Collegio**, where the doge and his inner cabinet met. Ruskin maintained that in no other part of the palace could you "enter so deeply into the heart of Venice", though he was referring not to the mechanics of Venetian power but to the luscious cycle of ceiling paintings by Veronese.

Next door – the **Sala del Senato** – was where most major policies were determined. A motley collection of late sixteenth-century artists produced the bombastic decoration of the walls and ceiling. Paolo Veronese again appears in the **Sala del Consiglio dei Dieci**, the room in which the much-feared Council of Ten discussed matters relating to state security. The unfortunates who were summoned before the Ten had to await their grilling in the next room, the **Sala della Bussola**; in the wall is a *Bocca di Leone* (Lion's Mouth), one of the boxes into which citizens could drop denunciations for the attention of the Ten and other state bodies.

Beyond the **armoury**, the Scala dei Censori takes you back to the second floor and the **Sala del Maggior Consiglio**, the assembly hall of all the Venetian patricians eligible to participate in the running of the city. This stupendous room, with its lavish ceiling, is dominated by the immense *Paradiso*, begun at the age of 77 by Tintoretto and completed by his son Domenico. Tintoretto was also commissioned to replace the room's frieze of portraits of the first 76 doges (the series continues in the Sala dello Scrutinio), but in the event Domenico and his assistants did the work.

THE PRISONS

A couple of rooms later, the route descends to the **Magistrato alle Leggi**, from where the Scala dei Censori leads to the **Ponte dei Sospiri** (Bridge of Sighs) and the **Prigioni** (Prisons). Built in 1600 by Antonio Contino, the bridge takes its popular name from the sighs of the prisoners who shuffled through its corridor. In reality, though, anyone passing this way had actually been let off pretty lightly. The hard cases were kept either in the sweltering **Piombi** (the Leads), under the roof of the Palazzo Ducale, or in the sodden gloom of the **Pozzi** (the Wells) in the bottom two storeys.

ARCADES OF THE PALAZZO DUCALE

THE VIEW FROM THE CAMPANILE

THE CAMPANILE

Daily: April–June & Oct 9am–7pm; July–Sept 9am–9pm; Nov–March 9am–3.45pm. €8.
MAP P.33, POCKET MAP G14

The Campanile began life as a combined lighthouse and belltower, and was continually modified up to 1515, the year in which the golden angel was installed on the summit. Each of its five **bells** had a distinct function: the *Marangona*, the largest, tolled the beginning and end of the working day; the *Trottiera* was a signal for

INSIDE THE CAMPANILE

members of the Maggior Consiglio to hurry along; the *Nona* rang midday; the *Mezza Terza* announced a session of the Senate; and the smallest, the *Renghiera* or *Maleficio*, gave notice of an execution. The Campanile played another part in the Venetian penal system – "persons of scandalous behaviour" ran the risk of being subjected to the *Supplizio della Cheba* (Torture of the Cage), which involved being stuck in a crate which was then hoisted up the south face of the tower. A more cheerful diversion was provided by the *Volo dell'Anzolo* or *del Turco* (Flight of the Angel or Turk), a stunt which used to be performed each year at the end of the Carnevale, in which an intrepid volunteer would slide on a rope from the top of the Campanile to the first-floor loggia of the Palazzo Ducale to present a bouquet to the doge.

But the Campanile's most dramatic contribution to the history of the city was made on July 14, 1902, the day on which, at 9.52am, it fell down. The town councillors decided that evening that the Campanile should be rebuilt "*dov'era e com'era*" (where it was and how it was), and a decade later, on St Mark's Day 1912, the new tower was opened, in all but minor details a replica of the original. At 99m, the Campanile is the tallest structure in the city, and from the top you can make out virtually every building, but not a single canal.

THE TORRE DELL'OROLOGIO

THE TORRE DELL'OROLOGIO

Daily 10am–5pm; tours in English Mon–Wed 10am & 11am, Thurs–Sun 2pm & 3pm; €12.50 (including Correr) or €7.50 with Museum Pass, and must be pre-booked on ☎041 520 9070, ✆torreorologio.visitmuve.it. MAP P.33, POCKET MAP G14

The other tower in the Piazza, the Torre dell'Orologio (Clock Tower), was built between 1496 and 1506. Legend relates that the makers of the clock slaved away for three years at their project, only to have their eyes put out so that they couldn't repeat their engineering marvel for other patrons. In fact the pair received a generous pension – presumably too dull an outcome for the city's folklorists. The bell on the tower's roof terrace is struck by two bronze wild men known as "The Moors", because of their dark patina. Almost completely replaced in the 1750s, the clock's mechanism has been frequently overhauled since – most recently (and controversially) during a decade-long restoration of the whole tower, which was finished in 2006. You can take an hour-long guided tour of the interior, which stops on each of the five floors to explicate the history and the workings of this complex machine.

THE PROCURATIE

MAP P.33, POCKET MAP G14–15

Away to the left of the Torre dell'Orologio stretches the **Procuratie Vecchie**, begun around 1500 to designs by Mauro Codussi, who also designed much of the clock tower. Once the home of the **Procurators of San Marco**, whose responsibilities included the upkeep of the Basilica and the administration of the other government-owned properties, the block earned substantial rents for the city coffers: the upper floors housed some of the choicest apartments in town, while the ground floor was leased to shopkeepers and craftsmen, as is still the case.

Within a century or so, the procurators were moved across the Piazza to new premises, the **Procuratie Nuove**. When Napoleon's stepson, Eugène Beauharnais, was the Viceroy of Italy, he appropriated this building as a royal palace, and then discovered that the accommodation lacked a ballroom. He duly demolished the church of San Geminiano, which had filled part of the third side of the Piazza, and connected the Procuratie Nuove and Vecchie with a new wing, the **Ala Napoleonica**, containing the essential facility.

THE CORRER AND ARCHEOLOGICAL MUSEUMS

Ⓦcorrer.visitmuve.it. Daily: April–Oct 10am–7pm; Nov–March 10am–5pm. Entrance with Museum Pass or San Marco museums card. MAP P.33, POCKET MAP G15

Many of the rooms in the Ala Napoleonica and Procuratie Nuove are now occupied by the **Museo Corror**, the chief civic museum of Venice, which is joined to the archeological museum and Sansovino's superb Libreria Sansoviniana.

Nobody could make out that the immense Correr collection is consistently fascinating, but it incorporates a picture gallery that more than makes up for the duller stretches, and its sections on Venetian society contain some eye-opening exhibits. You enter the Correr through the ballroom, where you'll see Canova's *Orpheus and Eurydice*, created when the sculptor was still in his teens. Then comes a suite of "Imperial rooms", which lead into a room in which you'll find Canova's *Venus Italica* and *Paris*: the pins in *Paris* were to enable Canova's assistants to map the coordinates onto the block of marble. Other pieces by Canova are on show in adjacent rooms, which you pass on your way out. After that you're into the historical collection, some of which will be enlightening only if you already have a pretty wide knowledge of Venetian history. In the nine-room "Wunderkammer Correr" scores of prints, paintings, books and objets d'art have been gathered into loosely thematic groupings. There are some beautiful items here, none more impressive than Jacopo de' Barbari's astonishing aerial view of Venice, engraved in 1500.

From here you pass directly into the Museo Archeologico, which is a somewhat scrappy museum, but look out for a head of Athena from the fourth century BC, a trio of wounded Gallic warriors (Roman copies of Hellenistic originals) and a phalanx of Roman emperors.

At the furthest point of the archeological museum a door opens into the hall of Sansovino's library (see p.42). Back in the Correr, a staircase beyond the sculpture section leads to the **Quadreria**, which may be no rival for the Accademia but nonetheless sets out clearly the evolution of painting in Venice from the thirteenth century to around 1500, and does contain some gems, including Jacopo de'Barbari's astonishing aerial view of Venice and a roomful of work by the Bellini family. The Correr's best-known possession, however, is the **Carpaccio** painting of two terminally bored women once known as *The Courtesans*, though in fact it depicts a couple of late fifteenth-century bourgeois ladies dressed in a style at which none of their contemporaries would have raised an eyebrow. The Correr also has a room of pictures from Venice's community of Greek artists, an immensely conservative group that nurtured the painter who later became known as El Greco – there's a picture by him here which you'd walk straight past if it weren't for the label.

From the Quadreria you might be directed to the **Museo del Risorgimento**, which resumes the history of the city with its fall to Napoleon, then the itinerary passes through sections on Venetian festivals, crafts, trades and everyday life. Here the frivolous items are what catch the eye, especially a pair of eighteen-inch stacked shoes, as worn by the women in the Carpaccio painting.

THE PIAZZETTA

MAP P.33, POCKET MAP G14–15

For much of the Republic's existence, the Piazzetta – the open space between the Basilica and the waterfront – was the area where the councillors of Venice would gather to scheme and curry favour. The Piazzetta was also used for public executions: the usual site was the pavement between the two granite columns on the Molo, as this stretch of the waterfront is called. The last person to be executed here was one Domenico Storti, condemned to death in 1752 for the murder of his brother.

One of the columns is topped by a modern copy of a statue of **St Theodore**, the patron saint of Venice when it was dependent on Byzantium; the original, now on show in a corner of one of the Palazzo Ducale's courtyards, was a compilation of a Roman torso, a head of Mithridates the Great, and miscellaneous bits and pieces carved in Venice in the fourteenth century (the dragon included).

The **winged lion** on the other column is an ancient 3000kg bronze beast that was converted into a lion of St Mark by jamming a Bible under its paws.

THE CAMPANILE

THE LIBRERIA SANSOVINIANA

Daily: April–Oct 10am–7pm; Nov–March 10am–5pm. Entrance with Museums Pass or San Marco museums card. MAP P.33. POCKET MAP G15

The Piazzetta is flanked by the Libreria Sansoviniana, also known as the Biblioteca Marciana. The impetus to build the library came from the bequest of Cardinal Bessarion, who left his celebrated hoard of classical texts to the Republic in 1468. Bessarion's books and manuscripts were first housed in San Marco and then in the Palazzo Ducale, but finally it was decided that a special building was needed. Jacopo Sansovino got the job, but the library wasn't finished until 1591, two decades after his death. Contemporaries regarded the Libreria as one of the supreme designs of the era, and the **main hall** is certainly one of the most beautiful rooms in the city: paintings by Veronese, Tintoretto, Andrea Schiavone and others cover the walls and ceiling.

DETAIL OF THE LIBRERIA SANSOVINIANA

THE ZECCA

MAP P.33, POCKET MAP G15

Attached to the Libreria, with its main facade to the lagoon, is Sansovino's first major building in Venice, the Zecca or Mint. Constructed in stone and iron to make it fireproof (most stonework in Venice is just skin-deep), it was built between 1537 and 1545 on the site occupied by the Mint since the thirteenth century. The rooms are now part of the library, but are not open to tourists.

THE GIARDINETTI REALI

MAP P.33, POCKET MAP G15

Beyond the Zecca, and behind a barricade of postcard and toy gondola sellers, is a small public garden – the Giardinetti Reali – created by Eugène Beauharnais on the site of the state granaries. It's the nearest place to the centre where you'll find a bench and the shade of a tree. The spruced-up building at the foot of the nearby bridge is the **Casino da Caffè**, another legacy of the Napoleonic era, the main tourist office before the current bout of restoration.

LIBRERIA SANSOVINIANA

Shops

MARTINUZZI

Piazza San Marco 67a. Mon–Sat 9am–7pm, plus March–Oct Sun 9.30am–7pm. MAP P.33, POCKET MAP G15

If cost is no object, call in at Martinuzzi, Venice's most durable and expensive purveyor of lace.

SEGUSO

Piazza San Marco 143 ⓦwww.3cguso.com Daily 10am–7pm. MAP P.33, POCKET MAP G14

Traditional-style Murano glass, much of it created by the firm's founder, Archimede Seguso.

VENINI

Piazzetta dei Leoncini 314 ⓦwww.venini .com. Mon–Sat 9.30am–5.30pm. MAP P.33, POCKET MAP G14

One of the more adventurous glass producers, Venini often employs designers from other fields of the applied arts.

Cafés and pasticcerie

FLORIAN

Piazza San Marco 56–59 ⓦcaffeflorian.com. Daily 9am–midnight; closed Tues in winter. MAP P.33, POCKET MAP G15

The most famous café in Venice began life in 1720, when Florian Francesconi's *Venezia Trionfante* (Venice Triumphant) opened for business here, though the gorgeous interior – a frothy confection of mirrors, stucco and frescoes – is a nineteenth-century pastiche. Its prices match its pedigree: a simple cappuccino at an outside table will set you back around €12, and you'll have to take out a mortgage for a cocktail; if the "orchestra" is playing, you'll be taxed another €6 for the privilege of hearing them. (*Quadri* and *Lavena* levy a similar surcharge.)

LAVENA

Piazza San Marco 133–134 ⓦlavena.it. Daily 9.30am–midnight; closed Tues in winter. MAP P.33, POCKET MAP G14

Wagner's favourite café (there's a commemorative plaque inside) is the second member of the Piazza's top-bracket trio. For privacy you can take a table in the narrow little gallery overlooking the bar. The coffee is in no way inferior to *Florian* or *Quadri*, and – unlike at *Florian* – you can keep down the price by drinking at the bar.

QUADRI

Piazza San Marco 120–124 ⓦalajmo.it. Daily 9am–midnight. MAP P.33, POCKET MAP G14

Quadri can claim an even longer lineage than *Florian*, as coffee has been on sale here since the seventeenth century, and it's in the same price league too. On the other hand, it's not quite as pretty, and its name doesn't have quite the same lustre, possibly because Austrian officers patronized it during the occupation, while the natives stuck with *Florian*.

FLORIAN

San Marco: north of the Piazza

From the Piazza the bulk of the pedestrian traffic flows north to the Rialto bridge along the Mercerie, the most browser-choked shopping mall in Venice. Only the churches of San Giuliano and San Salvador provide a diversion from the shops until you come to the Campo San Bartolomeo, the forecourt of the Rialto bridge and one of the locals' favoured spots for an after-work chat, along with the nearby Campo San Luca. Secreted in the folds of the alleyways hereabouts is the spiralling staircase called the Scala del Bovolo. And slotted away in a tiny square close to the Canal Grande you'll find the most delicate of Venice's museum buildings – the Palazzo Pésaro degli Orfei, home of the Museo Fortuny.

THE MERCERIE

MAP PP.46–47, POCKET MAP F12–G14

The Mercerie, a chain of streets that starts under the Torre dell'Orologio and finishes at the Campo San Bartolomeo, is the most direct route between San Marco and the Rialto and has always been a prime site for Venice's shopkeepers – its mixture of slickness and tackiness ensnares more shoppers than any other part of Venice. (Each of the five links in the chain is a *merceria*: Merceria dell'Orologio, di San Zulian, del Capitello, di San Salvador and 2 Aprile.) Keep your eye open for one quirky feature: over the Sottoportego del Cappello (first left after the Torre) is a relief known as **La Vecia del Morter** – the Old Woman of the Mortar. The event it commemorates happened on the night of June 15, 1310, when the occupant of this house, an old woman named Giustina Rossi, looked out of her window and saw a contingent of Bajamonte Tiepolo's rebel army passing below. Possibly by accident, she knocked a stone mortar from her sill, and the missile landed on the skull of the standard-bearer, killing him outright. Seeing their flag go down, Tiepolo's troops panicked and fled.

THE MERCERIE

SAN GIULIANO

Daily 9am–7pm. MAP PP.46–47, POCKET MAP G13

The church of San Giuliano or San Zulian, at the San Marco end of the Mercerie, was rebuilt in the mid-sixteenth century with the generous aid of the physician Tommaso Rangone. His munificence is attested by the Greek and Hebrew inscriptions on the facade and by Alessandro Vittoria's portrait statue above the door.

SAN SALVADOR

June–Aug. Mon–Sat 9am–noon & 4–7pm, Sun 4–7pm; Sept–May Mon–Sat 9am–noon & 3–7pm, Sun 3–7pm. PP.46–47, POCKET MAP F13

At its far end, the Mercerie veers right at the church of San Salvador or Salvatore, which was consecrated in 1177 by Pope Alexander III. The facade is less interesting than the interior, where, on the right-hand wall is Titian's *Annunciation* (1566), signed *"Fecit, fecit"* (Painted it, painted it) supposedly to emphasize the wonder of his continued creativity in extreme old age; a note on the rail in front of the picture records his death on August 25, 1576. Titian also painted the main altarpiece, a *Transfiguration*. The end of the right transept is filled by the **tomb** of **Caterina Cornaro**,

one of the saddest figures in Venetian history. Born into one of Venice's pre-eminent families, she became Queen of Cyprus by marriage, and after her husband's death was forced to surrender the strategically crucial island to the doge. On her return home she was led in triumph up the Canal Grande, as though her abdication had been voluntary, and then was presented with possession of the town of Ásolo as a token of gratitude. She died in 1510; this tomb was erected at the end of the century.

CAMPO SAN BARTOLOMEO

MAP PP.46–47, POCKET MAP F12

A popular spot for Venetians to meet friends, Campo San Bartolomeo, terminus of the Mercerie, comes to life in the evenings; the handful of bars scattered about, adds to the atmosphere. The **church of San Bartolomeo** (Tues, Thurs & Sat 10am–noon) has a landmark campanile, but its interior isn't thrilling: its organ panels, painted by Sebastiano del Piombo, are now housed in the Accademia, and its most famous picture, the altarpiece painted by Dürer at the request of the German merchant Christopher Fugger, long ago migrated to Prague.

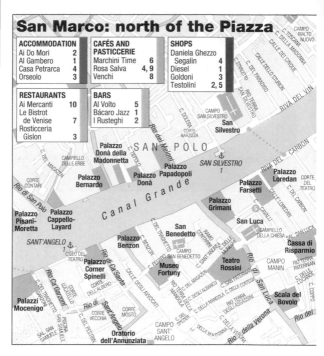

San Marco: north of the Piazza

ACCOMMODATION	
Ai Do Mori	2
Al Gambero	1
Casa Petrarca	4
Orseolo	3

CAFÉS AND PASTICCERIE	
Marchini Time	6
Rosa Salva	4, 9
Venchi	8

SHOPS	
Daniela Ghezzo	
Segalin	4
Diesel	1
Goldoni	3
Testolini	2, 5

RESTAURANTS	
Ai Mercanti	10
Le Bistrot de Venise	7
Rosticceria Gislon	3

BARS	
Al Volto	5
Bácaro Jazz	1
I Rusteghi	2

CAMPO SAN LUCA AND BACINO ORSEOLO

MAP ABOVE, POCKET MAP F13–14

If the crush of San Bartolomeo is too much for you, you can retire to **Campo San Luca** (past the front of San Salvador and straight on), another open-air social centre, with some good bars and cafés. From Campo San Luca, Calle Goldoni is a direct route back to the Piazza, via the **Bacino Orseolo** – the city's major gondola depot, and one of the few places where you can admire the streamlining and balance of the boats without being hassled.

CAMPO MANIN AND THE SCALA DEL BOVOLO

MAP ABOVE, POCKET MAP E14

Campo Manin – where, unusually, the most conspic-uous building is a modern one, Pier Luigi Nervi's Cassa di Risparmio di Venezia – was enlarged in 1871 to make room for the monument to Daniele Manin, the lawyer who was the leader of a revolt against the Austrians in

1848–49. On the wall of the alley on the south side of the campo, a sign directs you to the staircase known as the **Scala del Bovolo** (a *bovolo* is a snail shell in Venetian dialect). It was added to the Palazzo Contarini around 1500, perhaps to save some space indoors while also making an impression on the neighbours. At the moment the Scala del Bovolo is under restoration; once it's finished, it should be possible to go up the staircase – though the view of the staircase is perhaps more impressive than the view from it.

THE MUSEO FORTUNY

Campo San Benedetto ⓦ fortuny.visitmuve.it. Mon & Wed–Sun 10am–6pm. €10. MAP ABOVE. POCKET MAP D14

The Museo Fortuny is close at hand, hidden away in a campo

you'd never accidentally pass – take either of the bridges out of the Campo Manin, turn first right, and keep going. Born in Catalonia, **Mariano Fortuny** (1871–1949) is famous chiefly for the body-clinging silk dresses he created, which were so finely pleated that they could be threaded through a wedding ring, it was claimed. However, Fortuny was also a painter, architect, photographer, theatre designer and sculptor, and the contents of this rickety and atmospheric palazzo reflect his versatility, with ranks of exotic landscapes, pin-up nudes, terracotta portrait busts, stage machinery and so forth.

Design and photography exhibitions are held regularly in the museum, and how much of the building you get to see depends on how extensive the show is.

Shops

DANIELA GHEZZO SEGALIN

Calle dei Fuseri 4365 ⓦdanielaghezzo.it.
Mon–Fri 9.30am–12.30pm & 3.30–7.30pm, Sat
9am–12.30pm. MAP PP.46–47, POCKET MAP F14

Established in 1932 by Antonio
Segalin then run by his son
Rolando until 2003, this
workshop is now operated by
Rolando's star pupil Daniela
Ghezzo, who produces
wonderful handmade shoes,
from sturdy brogues to
whimsical Carnival footwear. A
pair of Ghezzos will set you
back at least €600.

DIESEL

Salizzada Pio X 5315–16 ⓦdiesel.com.
Mon–Sat 10am–7.30pm, Sun 11am–7pm.
MAP PP.46–47, POCKET MAP F12

Very few of the glitzy clothes
shops of the Mercerie have
much of a connection with
Venice or the Veneto, but there
are a few exceptions: Stefano
Gabbana (of Dolce e Gabbana)
is Venetian, the Benetton family
is from nearby Treviso, and
Renzo Rosso, the boss of Diesel,
was born near Padua. The Diesel
flagship store is, inevitably, in
Milan, but the Venice shop is
almost as good. The brand is
now huge, but denim is still
what it does best, and most of
the stuff is still made in Italy too.

GOLDONI

Calle dei Fabbri 4742. Mon 2–7pm, Tues–Sat
10am–7pm. MAP PP.46–47, POCKET MAP F13

The best general bookshop in
the city; also keeps a good
array of maps and posters.

TESTOLINI

Calle dei Fabbri 4744 Mon–Sat 9am–7.30pm;
Fondamenta Orseolo 1756, Mon–Sat
9am–1pm & 2.30–7pm. MAP PP.46–47,
POCKET MAP F13 & F14

The city's best-known
stationers, with a good range of

SIGN FOR ROSA SALVA

paper, pens, briefcases, etc. Art
materials are sold at the
Fondamenta Orseolo branch.

Cafés and pasticcerie

MARCHINI TIME

Campo San Luca 4589. Mon–Sat
7am–8.30pm. MAP PP.46–47, POCKET MAP E13

Sample the succulent *Marchini*
pastries with a cup of top-grade
coffee at this new, sleek café.

ROSA SALVA

Merceria S. Salvador 5020 and Calle Fiubera
951 ⓦwww.rosasalva.it. Mon–Sat 7.30am–
8.30pm. MAP PP.46–47, POCKET MAP F13 & G14

Excellent coffee and pastries –
but for a less businesslike
ambience, check out the
Zanipolo branch (see p.108).

VENCHI

Calle dei Fabbri 998a ☎ 041 241 2314,
ⓦvenchi.com. Sun–Thurs 10.30am–11pm,
Fri & Sat 10.30am–midnight. MAP PP.46–47,
POCKET MAP F14

Founded in Turin in 1878,
Venchi creates terrific
chocolates and ice cream – the
hazelnut gianduja is a
speciality.

Restaurants

AI MERCANTI

Corte Coppo 4346a ☎ 041 523 8269.
Ⓦaimercanti.it. Mon 7–10.30pm, Tues–Sat
12.30–3pm & 7–10.30pm. MAP PP.46–47,
POCKET MAP F14

Reinvented in 2013 as a
"*gastrosteria*", Ai Mercanti is one
of the few places in the San
Marco *sestiere* offering
good-quality and creative
cooking at prices that you
might describe as reasonable
– main courses start at around
€13. The menu is imaginative
(has anywhere else in Venice
served a pumpkin and coffee
bean risotto?), with more meat
than is the norm in Venice, and
also more vegetarian choices.
The dark wood and golden
colour scheme is distinctive too.

LE BISTROT DE VENISE

Calle dei Fabbri 4685 ☎ 041 523 6651.
Ⓦbistrotdevenise.com. Daily 11am–midnight.
MAP PP.46–47, POCKET MAP F13

Though done up as a facsimile
of a French bistro, the menu
here is based on old-style
Venetian recipes. You're paying
a premium for the location, but
the food is usually good, as is
the atmosphere, as *Le Bistrot* is
something of an arts centre,
with music and poetry every
Tuesday evening from October

to May. The bar closes at 1am,
the kitchen a half-hour earlier.
Main courses are €25–35, with
a set menu at around €65.

ROSTICCERIA GISLON

Calle della Bissa 5424a. Daily 9am–9.30pm.
MAP PP.46–47, POCKET MAP F12

Downstairs it's a sort of
glorified snack-bar, serving
pizzas and set meals starting
at around €12 – the trick is to
first grab a place at the tables
along the windows, then order
from the counter. Good if you
need to refuel quickly and
cheaply. There's a slightly less
rudimentary restaurant
upstairs, where prices are
considerably higher for no
great increase in quality.

Bars

AL VOLTO

Calle Cavalli 4081 Ⓦalvoltoenoteca.it.
Daily 10am–3pm & 6–11pm. MAP PP.46–47,
POCKET MAP E13

This dark little bar is an *enoteca*
in the true sense of the word
– 1300 wines from Italy and
elsewhere, 100 of them served
by the glass, some cheap, many
not; good snacks, too.

BÁCARO JAZZ

Salizzada Fondaco dei Tedeschi 5546
Ⓦbacarojazz.com. Daily 11am–2am.
MAP PP.46–47, POCKET MAP F12

A jazz-themed bar that's a big
hit with cool Venetian kids, not
least because of its late hours.

I RUSTEGHI

Corte del Tintor 5513. Mon–Sat 10.30am–
3pm & 6–9pm. MAP PP.46–47, POCKET MAP F12

Small *osteria*, secreted away in
a tiny courtyard close to
Campo San Bartolomeo. Great
cicheti, nice wine, congenial
host – plus a few outside tables.
The perfect place for a quiet
snack in the San Marco area.

AL VOLTO

San Marco: west of the Piazza

Leaving the Piazza by the west side you enter another major shopping district, where the clientele is drawn predominantly from Venice's well-heeled citizens or from the five-star tourists staying in the hotels that overlook the end of the Canal Grande. To a high proportion of visitors, this part of the city is principally the place to go for buying Gucci or Armani, or is merely the route to the Accademia, but there are things to see here apart from the latest creations from Milan and Paris – the extraordinary Baroque facades of Santa Maria del Giglio and San Moisè, for instance, or the graceful Santo Stefano, which rises at the end of one of the largest and most attractive squares in Venice.

SAN MOISÈ

Mon–Sat 9.30am–12.30pm. MAP PP.52–53. POCKET MAP F15

San Moisè, which was founded in the eighth century, would be the runaway winner of any poll for the ugliest church in Venice. The church's name means "Saint Moses", the Venetians here following the Byzantine custom of canonizing Old Testament figures, while simultaneously honouring Moisè Venier, who paid for a rebuilding way back in the tenth century. Its facade, featuring a species of camel unknown to zoology, was sculpted largely by Heinrich Meyring in 1668 and was financed by the Fini family, whose portraits occupy prime positions. If you think this bloated display of fauna and flora is in questionable taste, wait till you see the miniature mountain he carved as the main altarpiece, representing *Mount Sinai with Moses Receiving the Tablets*.

CALLE LARGA XXII MARZO

MAP PP.52–53. POCKET MAP E15–F15

If you're looking for €1000 handbag, or a €10,000 watch, or a new designer suit, then you'll probably find what you're

A VENETIAN *NIZIOLETO* OR STREET SIGN

after on or around the broad Calle Larga XXII Marzo, which begins over the canal from San Moisè. Many of the streets off the western side of the Piazza feature names such as Versace, Gucci, Ferragamo, Bulgari, Prada and Vuitton lurking around every corner.

LA FENICE

MAP PP52–53, POCKET MAP E15

Halfway along Calle Larga XXII Marzo, on the right, Calle del Sartor da Veste takes you over a canal and into **Campo San Fantin**. The square is dominated by the Teatro la Fenice, which is the oldest and largest theatre in Venice. Giannantonio Selva's gaunt Neoclassical design was not deemed a great success on its inauguration on December 26, 1792, but nonetheless very little of the exterior was changed when the place had to be rebuilt after a fire took place in 1836. Similarly, when La Fenice was again destroyed by fire on the night of January 29, 1996, it was decided to rebuild it as a replica of Selva's theatre: after all, its acoustics were superb and – with a capacity of just nine hundred people – it had an inspiringly intimate atmosphere. La Fenice saw some significant musical events in the twentieth century – Stravinsky's *The Rake's Progress* and Britten's *The Turn of the Screw* were both premiered here – but the music scene was more exciting in the nineteenth century, when, in addition to staging the premieres of operas by Rossini, Bellini and Verdi (*Rigoletto* and *La Traviata* both opened here), it became the focal point for a series of protests against the occupying Austrian army. For information on how to get tickets for performances, see p.57.

LA FENICE

SANTA MARIA DEL GIGLIO

Mon–Sat 10am–5pm. €3 or Chorus Pass.
MAP PP52–53, POCKET MAP E15

Back on the route to the Accademia, another extremely odd church awaits – Santa Maria del Giglio (Mary of the Lily), commonly known as Santa Maria Zobenigo, an alternative title derived from the name of the family who founded it in the ninth century. The exterior features not a single unequivocally Christian image: the main statues are of the five **Barbaro** brothers, who financed the rebuilding of the church in 1678; Virtue, Honour, Fame and Wisdom hover at a respectful distance; and relief maps at eye level depict the towns distinguished with the brothers' presence in the course of their military and diplomatic careers. The interior, full to bursting with devotional pictures and sculptures, overcompensates for the impiety of the exterior.

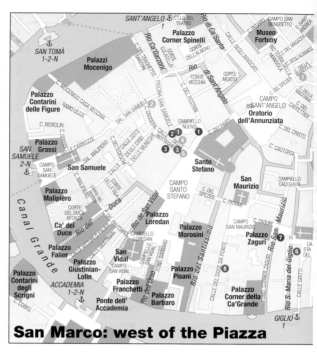

San Marco: west of the Piazza

SAN MAURIZIO AND THE SCUOLA DEGLI ALBANESI

San Maurizio daily 9.30am–7.30pm. MAP ABOVE.
POCKET MAP D15

The tilting campanile of **Santo Stefano** looms into view over the vapid and deconsecrated church of San Maurizio, which currently contains a display of Baroque musical instruments. A few metres away, at the head of Calle del Piovan, stands a diminutive building that was once the **Scuola degli Albanesi**, the confraternity of the city's Albanian community; it was established in 1497 and the reliefs on the facade date from shortly after that.

CAMPO SANTO STEFANO

MAP ABOVE, POCKET MAP D15

The church of Santo Stefano closes one end of the spacious Campo Santo Stefano. The campo has an alias – Campo Francesco Morosini – that comes from a former inhabitant of the **palazzo** at no. 2802. The last doge to serve as military commander of the Republic (1688–94), **Francesco Morosini** became a Venetian hero with his victories in the Peloponnese, but is notorious elsewhere as the man who lobbed a missile through the roof of the Parthenon, detonating the Turkish gunpowder barrels that had been stored there.

SANTO STEFANO

Mon–Sat 10am–5pm. Sacristy €3 or Chorus Pass. MAP ABOVE, POCKET MAP D14–15

The church of Santo Stefano is notable for its Gothic doorway and beautiful **ship's keel roof**, both of which date from the fifteenth century, the last phase of the church's construction.

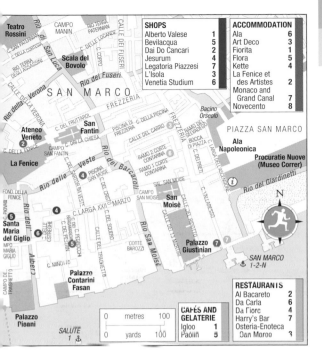

SHOPS	
Alberto Valese	1
Bevilacqua	5
Dai Do Cancari	2
Jesurum	4
Legatoria Piazzesi	7
L'Isola	3
Venetia Studium	6

ACCOMMODATION	
Ala	6
Art Deco	3
Fiorita	1
Flora	5
Kette	4
La Fenice et des Artistes	2
Monaco and Grand Canal	7
Novecento	8

RESTAURANTS	
Al Bacareto	2
Da Carla	6
Da Fiore	4
Harry's Bar	7
Osteria-Enoteca San Marco	3

CAFÉS AND GELATERIE	
Igloo	1
Paolin	5

The airy and calm interior is one of the most pleasant places in Venice just to sit and think, but it also contains some major works of art, notably in the picture-packed sacristy, where you'll find a *St Lawrence* and a *St Nicholas of Bari* by Bartolomeo Vivarini, a Crucifix by Paolo Veneziano, and a trio of late works by Tintoretto.

CAMPO SANTO STEFANO

CAMPIELLO NUOVO

MAP PP.52–53, POCKET MAP D14

Nearby Campiello Nuovo was formerly the churchyard of Santo Stefano, and was used as a burial pit during the catastrophic plague of 1630, which accounts for the square's peculiar raised pavement. Such was the volume of corpses interred here that for health reasons the site remained closed to the public from then until 1838.

PALAZZO PISANI

MAP PP.52–53, POCKET MAP E16

Campiello Pisani is a forecourt to the Palazzo Pisani, one of the biggest houses in the city, and now the Conservatory of Music. Work began on it in the early seventeenth century, continued for over a century, and was at last brought to a halt by the government, which decided that the Pisani, among the city's richest banking families, were getting ideas above their station. Had the Pisani got their way, they wouldn't have stopped building until they reached the Canal Grande.

SAN SAMUELE

MAP PP.52–53, POCKET MAP C15

From opposite the entrance to Santo Stefano church, Calle delle Botteghe and Crosera lead up to Salizzada San Samuele, a route that takes you past the house in which Paolo Veronese lived his final years, and on to **Campo San Samuele**. Built in the late twelfth century and not much altered since, the **campanile** of San Samuele is one of the oldest in the city. The church itself was largely reconstructed in the late seventeenth century.

PALAZZO GRASSI

Ⓦ www.palazzograssi.it. MAP PP.52–53, POCKET MAP C15

Dwarfing San Samuele is the Palazzo Grassi, which became famous in the twenty years it was run by Fiat for blockbusting exhibitions on subjects such as the Celts, the Pharaohs and the Phoenicians. In 2005 it was acquired by the phenomenally wealthy François Pinault, who has continued to use it as an exhibition space, often drawing on work from his own collection of contemporary art (see p.61).

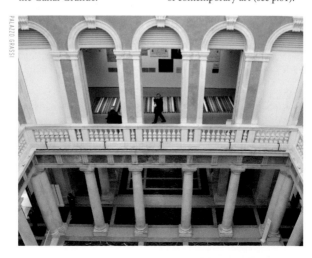

PALAZZO GRASSI

Shops

ALBERTO VALESE

Campo San Stefano 3471 ⓦ albertovalese
-ebru.it. Daily 10am–7pm. MAP PP.52–53,
POCKET MAP D14

Valese not only produces the
most luscious marbled papers
in Venice, but also transfers
the designs onto silk scarves
and a variety of ornaments; he
uses a Turkish marbling
technique called *ebrû* (meaning
cloudy) – hence the alternative
name of his shop (Ebrû).

BEVILACQUA

Campo Santa Maria del Giglio 2520
ⓦ bevilacquatessuti.com. Mon–Sat
10am–7pm, Sun 10am–5pm. MAP PP.52–53,
POCKET MAP E15

The Bevilacqua family has been
weaving silk in Venice since
around 1700, and the family
company – established in 1875
– is famed throughout Italy for
its patterned velvets, satins and
other luxurious materials.
Many of its fabrics are
manufactured using eight-
eenth-century weaving
techniques. Prices are
eye-popping – a single cushion
can cost more than €600.

DAI DO CANCARI

Calle delle Botteghe 3455.
Daily 10.30am–1pm & 3.30–7.45pm.
MAP PP.52–53, POCKET MAP D14

Perhaps Venice's best wine
shop, selling scores of Italy's
finest vintages, as well as cheap
draught wine (*vino sfuso*).

JESURUM

Calle Larga XXII Marzo 2401 ⓦ jesurum.it.
Tues–Sat 10am–5pm. MAP PP.52–53,
POCKET MAP E15

Renowned for its exquisite lace,
the long-established (but no
longer Venetian-owned)
Jesurum also produces

ALBERTO VALESE

luxurious bed linen, towels and
other fabrics.

L'ISOLA

Calle de le Botteghe 2970. Daily 9am–7pm.
MAP PP.52–53, POCKET MAP F15

Chiefly a showcase for work by
Carlo Moretti, the doyen of
modern Venetian glass artists.

LEGATORIA PIAZZESI

Campiello della Feltrina 2511
ⓦ legatoriapiazzesi.it. Mon–Sat 10am–1pm &
3–7pm. MAP PP.52–53, POCKET MAP D15

Located near Santa Maria del
Giglio, this paper-producer was
founded in 1851 and claims to
be the oldest such shop in Italy.
Using the wooden-block
method of printing, it makes
stunning hand-printed papers,
cards and pocket diaries.

VENETIA STUDIUM

Calle delle Ostreghe 2425 ⓦ venetiastudium
.com. Daily 11am–6pm. MAP PP.52–53, POCKET
MAP E15

Genuine Fortuny creations cost
a fortune, but this place sells
well-priced Fortuny-approved
replicas of lamps, bags and
scarves. There are other Venice
branches, the biggest of which
is in Dorsoduro, at Calle del
Bastion 186, between the
Guggenheim and the Salute.

Cafés and gelaterie

IGLOO

Calle della Mandola 3651. Daily: May–Sept 11am–8pm; Oct, Nov & Feb–April 11.30am–7.30pm; closed Jan & Dec.
MAP PP.52–53, POCKET MAP E14

Luscious home-made ice cream to take away – the summer fruit concoctions are especially delicious.

PAOLIN

Campo S. Stefano 2962. Daily 9am–10pm.
MAP PP.52–53, POCKET MAP D15

Campo Santo Stefano now has more cafés and restaurants than ever before, but *Paolin* has been here longer than any of them. In addition to drinks it serves some of the best ice cream in Venice, and the outside tables have a very nice setting.

Restaurants

AL BACARETO

Crosera 3447 ☎ 041 528 9336. Mon–Sat 8am–4.30pm & 6.30–11pm. MAP PP.52–53, POCKET MAP C14

Tucked away on the north side of Santo Stefano, *Al Bacareto* has been in business here for more than forty years and remains one of the most genuine and welcoming places in Venice's San Marco *sestiere*. In recent years it has been getting smarter and more expensive, but it's still good value, with main courses in the €15–20 range; if you're watching the pennies you can always eat at the bar, where the *cicheti* are outstanding. In the summer there is also seating outside.

DA CARLA

Sottoportego Corte Contarina 1535a
☎ 041 523 7855, ⓦosteriadacarla.it. Mon–Sat 8am–7pm. MAP PP.52–53, POCKET MAP F15

Hidden down a *sottoportego* off the west side of Frezzeria, *Da Carla* has a battered old sign that's rather misleading, as this place has been refashioned as a slick modern *osteria*. The menu is short but the food is well prepared, and the prices (pasta dishes around €10, main courses under €20) make this one of the best places for a simple meal close to the Piazza. The service – polite and attentive – is better than average for this part of town.

DA FIORE

Calle delle Botteghe 3461 ☎ 041 523 5310, ⓦdafiore.it. Mon & Wed–Sun 9am–10pm.
MAP PP.52–53, POCKET MAP D14.

This popular restaurant offers Venetian cuisine in a classy trattoria-style setting. The nice small bar offers good *cicheti* plus a small menu of daily specials – you might pay €15 for a fish dish in the bar section, and €25 for the same thing in the restaurant.

DA CARLA

HARRY'S BAR

Calle Vallaresso 1323 ☏ 041 528 5777,
Ⓦ cipriani.com. Daily 10.30am–11pm.
MAP PP.52-53, POCKET MAP F16

Harry's Bar is the most famous of Venice's gourmet restaurants (*carpaccio* – raw strips of thin beef – was first created here), though the place's reputation has as much to do with its exclusivity as with its cuisine. three courses will cost you around €130, and the cocktails and snacks are similarly insane. (The Bellini – a mix of fresh white peach juice and prosecco that's mistakenly thought by many to be a traditional Venetian drink – was invented here too.) *Harry's* was founded in 1931 by Giuseppe Cipriani, who named it after Harry Pickering, a young American who, by way of thanks for a loan that Cipriani had earlier given him to see him through a crisis, loaned Cipriani enough cash to set up his own bar. The Cipriani family continued to run the place until 2013, when, saddled with debts of several million euros, they were forced to cede control to an investment fund.

OSTERIA-ENOTECA SAN MARCO

Frezzeria 1610 ☏ 041 528 5242,
Ⓦ osteriasanmarco.it. Mon–Sat noon–11pm.
MAP PP.52-53, POCKET MAP F14

As you'd expect for a place so close to the Piazza, this classy modern *osteria* is far from cheap (expect to pay in the region of €25–30 for your main course), but the prices are not madly unreasonable for the quality of the food and location – and the wine list is very good. Between lunchtime and dinner you can sip wine at the bar.

Opera

LA FENICE

Campo San Fantin Ⓦ www.teatrolafenice.it.
MAP PP.52-53, POCKET MAP E15

The third-ranking Italian opera house after Milan's La Scala and Naples' San Carlo, La Fenice has opera and ballet performances throughout the year; classical concerts are held in the Fenice's Sale Apollinee. Seats for the opera cost €70–170 on most nights, but you'll pay rather more for the opening night of a production; prices are a little lower in mid-week than at the weekend, and restricted-view seats are sometimes available for as little as €15. Tickets can be bought online, at the Fenice box office and at the Venezia Unica/Hellovenezia offices at Piazzale Roma and the train station.

Dorsoduro

There weren't many places among the lagoon's mudbanks where Venice's early settlers could be confident that their dwellings wouldn't slither down into the water, but with Dorsoduro they were on relatively solid ground, it being the largest area of firm silt in the city's centre. The main draw here is the Gallerie dell'Accademia, the city's top art gallery, while the most conspicuous building is the huge Baroque church of Santa Maria della Salute. More notable for art, San Sebastiano was the parish church of Paolo Veronese, while Giambattista Tiepolo is represented at the Scuola Grande dei Carmini. Modern art is also in evidence – at the small yet impressive Guggenheim Collection and at the Punta della Dogana, home to the vast art collection of François Pinault.

THE ACCADEMIA

ⓦ gallerieaccademia.org. Mon 8.15am–2pm, Tues–Sun 8.15am–7.15pm. €9 includes admission to Palazzo Grimani. MAP PP.60–61, POCKET MAP C16

The **Accademia** is one of Venice's obligatory tourist sights, but admission is restricted to three hundred people at a time, so if you're visiting in high summer get there well before the doors open. A recent expansion of the galleries will entail a rehang, with the upper floors focusing on art up to the seventeenth century, with the new lower galleries featuring later artists. This means that the layout will soon be somewhat different than the sequence given below.

The first room is filled with pieces by the earliest-known individual Venetian painters, Paolo Veneziano and his follower Lorenzo Veneziano. Beyond here, room 2 is given over to large altarpieces from the late fifteenth and early sixteenth centuries, including works by Giovanni Bellini, Cima da Conegliano and Vittore Carpaccio. Carpaccio's strange *Crucifixion and Glorification of the Ten Thousand Martyrs of Mount Ararat* is the room's most gruesome painting, and the most charming is by him too: *The Presentation of Jesus in the Temple*, with its wingless, lute-playing angel.

The emergence of the characteristically soft and rich Venetian palette is seen in rooms 3, 4 and 5, the last two of which are a high point of the Accademia. Outstanding are a series of *Madonnas* and a *Pietà* by **Giovanni Bellini**, and two pieces by **Giorgione** – his *Portrait of an Old Woman* and the so-called *Tempest* (c.1500).

Rooms 6 to 8 mark the entry of Tintoretto, Titian and Veronese, while in room 10, one whole wall is needed for *Christ in the House of Levi* by **Paolo Veronese**. Originally called *The Last Supper*, this picture brought down on Veronese the wrath of the

Inquisition; Inquisitors objected to the inclusion of "buffoons, drunkards, Germans, dwarfs, and similar indecencies" in the sacred scene. Veronese's insouciant response was simply to change the title. Among **Tintoretto**'s works is the painting that made his reputation: *St Mark Freeing a Slave* (1548), showing St Mark's intervention at the execution of a slave who had defied his master by travelling to the Evangelist's shrine. Opposite is **Titian**'s *Pietà* (1576), painted for his own tomb in the Frari and completed after his death by Palma il Giovane.

In room 11 a major shift into the eighteenth century occurs, with pieces by **Giambattista Tiepolo**; his contemporaries provide the chief interest of the next section, with works such as **Giambattista Piazzetta**'s extraordinary *The Fortune-Teller*, **Guardi**'s views of Venice, **Pietro Longhi**'s interiors and a

series of portraits by **Rosalba Carriera**, one of the very few women shown in the collection.

After a large hall that houses numerous paintings by two of Venice's most significant artistic dynasties, the **Vivarini** and **Bellini** families, you come to room 20, which is entirely filled by the cycle *The Miracles of the Relic of the Cross*. Produced by various artists (most notably Gentile Bellini) between 1494 and 1501, it was commissioned by the Scuola Grande di San Giovanni Evangelista.

Another remarkable cycle fills room 21 – **Carpaccio**'s *Story of St Ursula*, painted for the Scuola di Sant'Orsola at San Zanipolo in 1490–94. A superlative exercise in pictorial narrative, the paintings are a record of Venice's domestic architecture and costume at the close of the fifteenth century. After this, you leave the Accademia through a door beneath **Titian**'s *Presentation of the Virgin* (1539), still occupying the space for which it was painted.

DETAIL OF VERONESE'S CHRIST IN THE HOUSE OF LEVI

Dorsoduro

ACCOMMODATION

Accademia	
Villa Maravege	4
Agli Alboretti	6
American Dinesen	8
Ca' Maria Adele	9
Ca' Pisani	7
DD 724	5
Fujiyama	3
La Calcina	11
Locanda	
San Barnaba	2
Messner	10
Pausania	1

THE GUGGENHEIM

Ⓦ guggenheim-venice.it. Mon & Wed–Sun 10am–6pm. €12. MAP ABOVE, POCKET MAP D16

Until François Pinault came to town, the city's most famous showing of modern art was the Peggy **Guggenheim Collection**, which is installed in the quarter-built **Palazzo Venier dei Leoni**, a bit farther up the Canal Grande from the Accademia.

In the early years of the twentieth century the leading lights of the Futurist movement came here for the parties thrown by the dotty Marchesa Casati, who was fond of stunts like setting wild cats and apes loose in the palazzo garden, among plants sprayed lilac for the occasion. Peggy Guggenheim, a considerably more discerning patron of the arts, moved into the palace in 1949; since her death in 1979 the Guggenheim Foundation has administered the place, and has turned her private collection into one of the city's glossiest museums – and the second most popular after the Accademia. It's a small but generally top-quality assembly of twentieth-century art and a prime venue for touring exhibitions. In the permanent collection the core pieces include Brancusi's *Bird in Space* and *Maestra*, De Chirico's *Red Tower* and *Nostalgia of the Poet*, Max Ernst's *Robing of the Bride* (Guggenheim was married to Ernst in the 1940s), sculpture by Laurens and Lipchitz, and works by Malevich and Schwitters; other artists include Picasso, Braque, Chagall, Pollock, Duchamp, Giacometti, Picabia and Magritte. Marino Marini's *Angel of the Citadel*,

SHOPS	
Antichità Zaggia	6
Ca' Macana	4
Il Grifone	1
Il Pavone	7
Libreria della Toletta	5
Paolo Olbi	2
Perlamadre	3

CAFÉS AND PASTICCERIE	
Il Caffè	6
Il Doge	9
Majer	10
Nico	16
Tonolo	3

BARS AND SNACKS	
Ai Do Draghi	5
Café Noir	1
Cantina del Vino già Schiavi	15
Da Còdroma	11
Impronta Cafè	4
Margaret DuChamp	8
Osteria alla Bifora	7
Vinus Venezia	2

RESTAURANTS	
Ai Quattro Ferri	13
La Bitta	14
La Piscina	17
Oniga	12

out on the terrace, flaunts his erection at the passing canal traffic; more decorous pieces by Giacometti, Moore, Paolozzi and others are planted in the garden, surrounding Peggy Guggenheim's burial place.

THE PUNTA DELLA DOGANA

ⓦ www.palazzograssi.it. Mon & Wed–Sun 10am–7pm. €15, or €20 with Palazzo Grassi. MAP ABOVE, POCKET MAP F16

The Punta della Dogana occupies the Dogana di Mare, the city's old customs house, which lies in the shadow of the Salute church, at the tip of the Canal Grande. In 2009 this was converted into a showcase for the colossal art collection of François Pinault, the co-owner of Palazzo Grassi (see p.54). Hundreds of works are on display at any one time, and as Pinault has invested in most of the really big names of the current art scene, you can expect to see pieces by the likes of Cindy Sherman, Luc Tuymans, Cy Twombly, Thomas Schütte, Maurizio Cattelan, Jeff Koons, the Chapman brothers and Marlene Dumas.

THE PUNTA DELLA DOGANA

DORSODURO

SANTA MARIA DELLA SALUTE

Daily 9am–noon & 3–6pm. MAP PP.60–61.
POCKET MAP E16

In 1630–31 Venice was devastated by a plague that exterminated nearly 95,000 of the lagoon's population – one person in three. In October 1630 the Senate decreed that a new church would be dedicated to Mary if the city were saved, and the result was Santa Maria della Salute (*salute* meaning "health" and "salvation"). Resting on a platform of more than one hundred thousand wooden piles, the Salute took half a century to build; its architect, **Baldassare Longhena**, was only 26 years old when his proposal was accepted and lived just long enough to see it finished, in 1681.

Each year on November 21 (the feast of the Presentation of the Virgin) the Signoria is processed from San Marco to the Salute for a service of thanksgiving, crossing the Canal Grande on a pontoon bridge laid from Santa Maria del Giglio. The Festa della Madonna della Salute is still a major event in the Venetian calendar.

The form of the Salute is replete with Marian symbolism: the octagonal plan and eight facades allude to the eight-pointed Marian star, for example, while the huge dome represents Mary's crown and the centralized plan is a conventional symbol of the Virgin's womb. Less arcane symbolism is at work on the **high altar**, where the Virgin and Child rescue Venice (kneeling woman) from the plague (old woman); in

SANTA MARIA DELLA SALUTE

attendance are saints Mark and Lorenzo Giustiniani, first Patriarch of Venice.

The most notable paintings in the Salute are the **Titian** pieces brought from the suppressed church of Santo Spirito in Isola in 1656, and now displayed in the sacristy (€3). Tintoretto has included himself in the dramatis personae of his *Marriage at Cana* (1561) – he's the first Apostle on the left.

THE ZÁTTERE

MAP PP.60–61, POCKET MAP C7–G7

Known collectively as the **Záttere**, the sequence of waterfront pavements between the Punta della Dogana and the Stazione Maríttima are now a popular place for a stroll or a waterside meal, but were formerly the place where most of the bulky goods coming into Venice were unloaded onto floating rafts called *záttere*.

THE GESUATI

Mon–Sat 10am–5pm. €3 or Chorus Pass.
MAP PP.60–61, POCKET MAP E8

As you walk along the Záttere from the mouth of the Canal Grande, the first building to break your stride is the church of the **Gesuati** or Santa Maria del Rosario. Rebuilt in 1726–43, about fifty years after the church was taken over from the order of the Gesuati by the Dominicans, this was the first church designed by **Giorgio Massari**, an architect who often worked with **Giambattista Tiepolo**. Tiepolo painted the first altarpiece on the right, *The Virgin with SS. Catherine of Siena, Rose and Agnes* (c.1740), and the three magnificent ceiling panels, *Scenes from the Life of St Dominic* (1737–39), which are seen to best effect in the afternoon. The third altar on this side of the church is adorned with the painting *SS. Vincent Ferrer, Giacinto and Luigi Beltran* by Tiepolo's principal forerunner, Giambattista Piazzetta; opposite, the first altar has Sebastiano Ricci's *Pius V with SS. Thomas Aquinas and Peter Martyr* (1739), completing the church's array of Rococo propaganda on behalf of the exalted figures of Dominican orthodoxy, followed by a tragically intense *Crucifixion* by Tintoretto (c.1555) on the third altar.

SAN TROVASO

Mon–Sat 2.30–5.30pm. MAP PP.60–61.
POCKET MAP B16

Don't bother consulting your dictionary of saints for the dedicatee of **San Trovaso** church – the name's a baffling dialect version of Santi Gervasio e Protasio. Since its tenth-century foundation the church has had a chequered history, falling down once, and twice being destroyed by fire; this is the fourth incarnation, built from 1584 to 1657.

Venetian folklore has it that this church was the only neutral ground between the Nicolotti and the Castellani, the two factions into which the working-class citizens of the city were divided – the former, coming from the west and north of the city, were named after the church of San Nicolò dei Mendicoli (see p.66), the latter, from the *sestieri* of Dorsoduro, San Marco and Castello, took their name from San Pietro di Castello. The rivals celebrated inter-marriages and other services here, but are said to have entered and departed by separate doors.

Inside, San Trovaso is spacious and somewhat characterless, but it does boast a pair of fine paintings by **Tintoretto**: *The Temptation of St Anthony*, in the chapel to the left of the high altar, and *The Last Supper* in the chapel at ninety degrees to it.

THE SQUERO DI SAN TROVASO

MAP PP.60–61. POCKET MAP B16/D8

Ten thousand gondolas operated on the canals of sixteenth-century Venice, when they were the standard form of transport to get around the city; nowadays the tourist trade is pretty well all that sustains the city's fleet of around five hundred boats, which provide steady employment for a couple

Gondolas

The earliest mention of a gondola is in a decree of 1094, but the vessel of that period bore little resemblance to today's streamlined thoroughbred. As late as the thirteenth century the gondola was a twelve-oared beast with an iron beak – an adornment that evolved into the saw-toothed projection called the **ferro**, which fronts the modern gondola. Over the next two centuries the gondola shrank to something near its present dimensions, developed multicoloured coverings and sprouted the little chair on carved legs that it still carries. The gondola's distinctive oarlock, an elaborately convoluted lump of walnut or cherry wood known as a **forcola**, which permits the long oar to be used in eight different positions, reached something like its present form at this time too.

There's been little alteration in the gondola's dimensions and construction since the end of the seventeenth century: the only significant changes have been adjustments of the gondola's asymmetric line to compensate for the weight of the gondolier. All gondolas are 10.87m long and 1.42m wide at their broadest point, and are assembled from nearly three hundred pieces of seasoned mahogany, elm, oak, lime, walnut, fir, cherry and larch. Gondolas are regularly brought into the boatyards for repair, but each *squero* turns out only about four new gondolas a year.

of **squeri**, as the gondola yards are called. A display in the Museo Storico Navale (see p.113) takes you through the construction of a gondola, but no abstract demonstration can equal the fascination of a working yard, and the most public one in Venice is the *squero* di San Trovaso, on the Záttere side of San Trovaso church. The San Trovaso *squero* was established in the seventeenth century and looks rather like an alpine farmhouse, a reflection of the architecture of the Dolomite villages from which many of Venice's gondola-builders once came.

SAN SEBASTIANO

Mon–Sat 10am–5pm, €3 or Chorus Pass.
MAP PP.60–61, POCKET MAP C7

At the end of the Záttere the barred gates of the Stazione Maríttima deflect you away from the waterfront and towards the church of San Sebastiano. The parish church of **Paolo Veronese**, it contains a group of resplendent paintings by him that gives it a place in his career comparable to that of San Rocco in the career of Tintoretto, but the church attracts nothing like the number of visitors that San Rocco gets.

Veronese was still in his twenties when, thanks largely to his contacts with the Verona-born prior of San Samuele, he was asked to paint the ceiling of the **sacristy** with a *Coronation of the Virgin* and the *Four Evangelists* (1555); once that commission had been carried out, he decorated the **nave ceiling** with *Scenes from the Life of St Esther*. His next project, the dome of the chancel, was later destroyed, but the sequence he and his brother Benedetto then painted on the walls of the church and the nun's choir at the end of the 1550s has survived in pretty good shape. In the following decade he executed the last of the pictures, those on the **organ shutters** and around the **high altar** – on the left, *St Sebastian Leads SS Mark and Marcellian to Martyrdom*, and on the right, *The Second Martyrdom of St Sebastian*. Other riches include a late **Titian**, *St Nicholas* (on the left wall of the first chapel on the right), and the early sixteenth-century majolica pavement in the Cappello Lando, to the left of the chancel – in front of which is Veronese's tomb slab.

GONDOLAS AT THE SQUERO DI SAN TROVASO

ANGELO RAFFAELE

Mon–Sat 8am–noon & 3–5.30pm, Sun 9am–noon. MAP PP.60–61. POCKET MAP B7

On the far side of Campo San Sebastiano, the seventeenth-century church of **Angelo Raffaele** is instantly recognizable by the two huge war memorials blazoned on the canal facade. Inside, the organ loft above the entrance on the canal side is decorated with *Scenes from the Life of St Tobias*, painted by one or other of the **Guardi** brothers (nobody's sure which). Although small in scale, the free brushwork and imaginative composition make the panels among the most charming examples of Venetian Rococo, a fascinating counterpoint to the grander visions of Giambattista Tiepolo, the Guardis' brother-in-law.

SAN NICOLÒ DEI MENDICOLI

Daily 10am–noon & 4–6pm. MAP PP.60–61. POCKET MAP B7

Although it's located on the edge of the city, the church of **San Nicolò dei Mendicoli** is one of Venice's oldest, said to have been founded in the seventh century. Its long history was reflected in the

fact that it gave its name to the **Nicolotti** faction, whose titular head, the so-called *Gastaldo* or the *Doge dei Nicolotti*, was elected by the parishioners and then honoured by a ceremonial greeting from the Republic's doge.

The church has been rebuilt and altered at various times, and was last restored in the 1970s, when Nic Roeg used it as a setting for *Don't Look Now*. In essence, however, its shape is still that of the Veneto-Byzantine structure raised here in the twelfth century, the date of its rugged campanile. The other conspicuous feature of the exterior is the fifteenth-century porch, a type of construction once common in Venice, and often used here as makeshift accommodation for penurious nuns. The **interior** is a miscellany of periods and styles. Parts of the apse and the columns of the nave go back to the twelfth century, but the darkened gilded woodwork that gives the interior its rather overcast appearance was installed late in the sixteenth century, as were most of the paintings, many of which were painted by Alvise dal Friso and other pupils of Paolo Veronese.

CAMPO DI SANTA MARGHERITA

MAP PP.60–61, POCKET MAP A14

Campo di Santa Margherita is the social heart of Dorsoduro, and is one of the most appealing squares in the whole city. The Piazza San Marco nowadays is overrun with tourists, but Campo di Santa Margherita – the largest square on this side of the Canal Grande – belongs to the Venetians and retains a spirit of authenticity. Ringed by houses that date back as far as the fourteenth century, it's spacious

SAN NICOLÒ DEI MENDICOLI

and at the same time modest, taking its tone not from any grandiose architecture (it's one of very few squares with no *palazzo*), but from its cluster of market stalls and its plethora of bars and cafés, which draw a lot of their custom from the nearby university.

SAN PANTALEONE

Mon–Sat 10am noon and 1–3pm. MAP PP.60–61, POCKET MAP A13–14

The church of San Pantaleone, to the north of Campo di Santa Margherita, has the most melodramatic **ceiling** in Venice. Painted on sixty panels, some of which jut out over the nave, *The Martyrdom and Apotheosis of St Pantaleone* kept **Gian Antonio Fumiani** busy from 1680 to 1704. Sadly, he never got the chance to bask in the glory of his labours – he died in a fall from the scaffolding from which he'd been working. In addition, the church possesses a fine picture by Antonio Vivarini and Giovanni d'Alemagna (in the chapel to the left of the chancel) and Veronese's last painting, *St Pantaleone Healing a Boy* (second chapel on right).

THE CARMINI SCUOLA AND CHURCH

ⓦwww.scuolagrandecarmini.it. Scuola: daily 11am–4pm; €5. Church: Mon–Sat 2.30–5.30pm. MAP PP.60–61, POCKET MAP C6

Just off Campo di Santa Margherita's southwest tip is the **Scuola Grande dei Carmini**, once the Venetian base of the Carmelites. Originating in Palestine towards the close of the twelfth century, the Carmelites blossomed during the Counter-Reformation, when they became the shock-troops through whom the cult of the Virgin could be disseminated. The Venetian Carmelites became immensely wealthy, and in the 1660s they called in an architect – probably Longhena – to re-design the property they had acquired. The core of this complex is now effectively a showcase for the art of **Giambattista Tiepolo**, who in the 1740s painted the wonderful ceiling of the upstairs hall.

The adjacent **Carmini** church, or Santa Maria del Carmelo, is a collage of architectural styles, with a sixteenth-century facade, a Gothic side doorway which preserves several Byzantine fragments, and a fourteenth-century basilican interior. A dull series of Baroque paintings illustrating the history of the Carmelite order covers a lot of space inside, but the second altar on the right has a *Nativity* by Cima da Conegliano (before 1510), and Lorenzo Lotto's *SS. Nicholas of Bari, John the Baptist and Lucy* (1529) – featuring what Bernard Berenson ranked as one of the most beautiful landscapes in all Italian art – hangs on the opposite side of the nave.

DORSODURO

THE PONTE DEI PUGNI

MAP PP.60–61, POCKET MAP A15

Cutting down the side of the Carmini church takes you over the Rio di San Barnaba, along which a *fondamenta* runs to the church of San Barnaba. Just before the end of the *fondamenta* you pass the Ponte dei Pugni, one of several bridges with this name. Originally built without parapets, they were the sites of ritual battles between the Castellani and Nicolotti; this one is inset with marble footprints marking the starting positions. These massed brawls took place between September and Christmas, and obeyed a well-defined etiquette, with prescribed ways of issuing challenges and deploying the antagonists prior to the outbreak of hostilities, the aim of which was to gain possession of the bridge. The fights themselves, however, were sheer bedlam, and fatalities were commonplace, as the armies slugged it out with bare knuckles and steel-tipped lances made from hardened rushes. The lethal weaponry was outlawed in 1574, after a particularly bloody engagement that was arranged for the visit of Henry III of France, and in 1705 the punch-ups were finally banned, and less dangerous forms of competition, such as regattas, were encouraged instead.

SAN BARNABA

MAP PP.60–61, POCKET MAP B15

The huge, damp-ridden San Barnaba church, built in 1749, has a trompe l'oeil ceiling painting of *St Barnabas in Glory* by Constantino Cedini, a follower of Tiepolo. Despite recent restoration, the ceiling is being restored again because of moisture damage; while that's going on, the church has been turned over to an exhibition on the "machines of Leonardo".

CA' REZZONICO

ⓦ carezzonico.visitmuve.it. Mon & Wed–Sun: April–Oct 10am–6pm; Nov–March 10am–5pm. €10 or Museum Pass. MAP PP.60–61, POCKET MAP B15

The **Museo del Settecento Veneziano** – The Museum of the Venetian Eighteenth Century – spreads through most of the enormous Ca' Rezzonico, a palazzo that the city authorities bought in 1934 specifically as a home for the museum. It's never been one of

GROCERY BARGE AT THE PONTE DEI PUGNI

the most popular of Venice's museums, but a recently completed renovation might go some way to rectifying its unjustified neglect.

A man in constant demand in the early part of the eighteenth century was the Belluno sculptor-cum-woodcarver **Andrea Brustolon**, much of whose output consisted of wildly elaborate pieces of furniture, exemplified by the stuff on show in the Brustolon Room. The less fervid imaginations of **Giambattista Tiepolo** and his son **Giandomenico** are introduced in room 2 with the ceiling fresco celebrating Ludovico Rezzonico's marriage into the hugely powerful Savorgnan family in 1758. Beyond room 4, with its array of pastels by **Rosalba Carriera**, you come to two other Tiepolo ceilings, enlivening the rooms overlooking the Canal Grande on each side of the main portego – an *Allegory of Merit* by Giambattista and Giando-

menico, and *Nobility and Virtue Triumphing over Perfidy*, a solo effort by the father.

In the portego of the second floor hang the only two canal views by **Canaletto** on show in public galleries in Venice. The next suite of rooms contains the museum's most engaging paintings – Giandomenico Tiepolo's sequence of **frescoes from the Villa Zianigo** near Mestre, the Tiepolo family home. Begun in 1759, the frescoes were completed towards the end of the century, by which time Giandomenico's style was going out of fashion. There's an air of wistful melancholy in pictures such as *The New World* (1791), which shows a crowd turned out in its best attire at a Sunday fair. The following rooms display delightful portraits and depictions of everyday Venetian life by **Francesco Guardi** (including high-society recreation in the parlour of San Zaccaria's convent) and **Pietro Longhi**, whose artlessly candid work – such as a version of the famous *Rhinoceros* – has more than enough curiosity value to make up for its shortcomings in execution.

The low-ceilinged rooms of the third and fourth floor contain the Pinacoteca Egidio Martini, a large but rarely thrilling private donation of Venetian art from the fifteenth to twentieth centuries, but you do get a tremendous view across the rooftops from here, and there's one unusual exhibit: an old **pharmacy**, comprising a sequence of wood-panelled rooms heavily stocked with ceramic jars and glass bottles. Back on the ground floor, steps lead up to the Mestrovich collection, which is smaller and even less engrossing than the Martini bequest.

Shops

ANTICHITÀ ZAGGIA

Calle Toletta 1195/a. Mon–Sat 9.30am–1pm
& 3.30–7pm. MAP PP.60–61, POCKET MAP B16

Period jewellery and new items
made with tiny antique beads,
which can also be bought
individually.

CA' MACANA

Calle delle Botteghe 3172 ⓦ camacana.com.
Daily 10am–6pm. MAP PP.60–61, POCKET MAP B15

Terrific mask shop-cum-studio,
with perhaps the biggest stock
in the city; it has another
branch on the other side of
Campo San Barnaba, at
Barbaria delle Tole 1169.

IL GRIFONE

Fondamenta del Gaffaro 3516 ⓦ ilgrifone
venezia.it. Tues–Fri 9am–12.30pm & 4–7.30pm,
Sat 10am–noon. MAP PP.60–61, POCKET MAP C5

Handmade briefcases, satchels,
purses, belts and other pieces
made from beautifully soft
leather. Reasonable prices.

IL PAVONE

Fondamenta Venier 721. Daily
9.30am–1.30pm & 2.30–6.30pm. MAP PP.60–61,
POCKET MAP D16

Nice wooden-block printed
papers, folders and so on, plus
an interesting line in
personalized rubber stamps
and *Ex Libris* bookplates.

LIBRERIA DELLA TOLETTA

Sacca della Toletta 1214 ⓦ libreriatoletta.it.
July & Aug Mon–Sat 9.30am–1pm &
3.30–7.30pm; rest of year Mon–Sat
9.30am–7.30pm, Sun 3.30–7.30pm. MAP
PP.60–61, POCKET MAP B16

Sells reduced-price books,
mainly in Italian, but some
dual-language and translations;
keeps a good stock of
Venice-related titles. Two
adjacent branches sell art,
architecture, design and
photography titles.

PAOLO OLBI

Ponte Ca' Fóscari 3253, Dorsoduro ☎ 041
523 7655. Daily 10.30am–12.30pm &
3.30–7.30pm. MAP PP.60–61. POCKET MAP B14

The founder of this
bookbindery and stationery
shop was largely responsible for
the revival of paper marbling in
Venice; today Olbi sells a range
of marbled notebooks, diaries
and other paper goods from his
workshop by the entrance to
the main university building.

PERLAMADRE

Calle delle Botteghe 3182 ☎ 340 844 9112,
ⓦ perlamadredesign.com. Mon–Sat
10.30am–1pm & 3.30–6pm. MAP PP.60–61.
POCKET MAP B15

Patrizia Iacovazzi makes
wonderful pieces of bold glass
jewellery in her tiny Dorsoduro
workshop; earrings from around
€30, necklaces from €80.

IL GRIFONE

Cafés and pasticcerie

IL CAFFÈ

Campo S. Margherita 2963 🌐 cafferosso
.it. Mon–Sat 7am–1am. MAP PP.60–61, POCKET
MAP A14

Known as *Caffè Rosso* for
its big red sign, this small,
atmospheric, old-fashioned
café-bar is a big student
favourite. Serves good
sandwiches, and there are
lots of seats outside in the
campo.

IL DOGE

Campo S. Margherita 3058. Daily 10am–
midnight, but often closes earlier. Closed Nov
& Dec. MAP PP.60–61, POCKET MAP A15

Well-established, very friendly
and extremely good hole-in-
the-wall *gelateria*, which also
does a superb granita, made in
the traditional Sicilian way.

MAJER

Rio Terrà Canal 3108b 🌐 majer.it. Mon–Sat
7.15am–8pm, Sun 8.30am–8pm. MAP PP.60–61,
POCKET MAP A15

Founded as a bakery back in
1924, *Majer* has opened this
functional yet pleasant café
on the south side of Campo
Santa Margherita. Their
pastries are as good as their
bread, and the coffee is fine.
At the moment *Majer* has half
a dozen other branches in
Venice, and there may be
more on the way.

NICO

Zàttere ai Gesuati 922. Mon–Wed & Fri–Sun
6.45am–10pm. MAP PP.60–61, POCKET MAP D8

This *café-gelateria*, which has
been in existence for more
than seventy years, is
celebrated for an artery-
clogging creation called a
gianduiotto da passeggio – a
paper cup with a block of
praline ice cream drowned in
whipped cream. Also boasts
lovely waterfront views.

TONOLO

Crosera 3764. Tues–Sat 7.45am–8pm, Sun
7.45am–1pm. MAP PP.60–61, POCKET MAP B13

One of the busiest cafés on one
of the busiest streets of the
student district, especially
hectic on Sunday mornings,
when the fancy *Tonolo* cakes
are in high demand. Don't miss
their sweet, almond-encrusted
Focaccia di Venezia.

Restaurants

AI QUATTRO FERRI

Calle Lunga S. Barnaba 2754a ☎041 520 6978.
Mon-Sat 12.30-3.30pm & 7-10.30pm. No credit
cards. MAP PP.60-61, POCKET MAP A15

A very highly recommended
osteria just off Campo San
Barnaba with a menu that
changes daily but often
consists entirely of fish and
seafood. Booking essential at
all times.

LA BITTA

Calle Lunga S. Barnaba 2753a ☎041 523
0531. Mon-Sat 6.30-11pm. No credit cards.
MAP PP.60-61, POCKET MAP A15

Innovative menu that's
remarkable for featuring
hardly anything aquatic.
Marcellino runs the kitchen
while his wife Debora serves
the guests, offering expert
guidance on the impressive
wine and grappa list. Delicious
cheese platter, served with
honey and fruit chutney. Tiny
dining room and garden;
booking essential.

LA PISCINA

Záttere ai Gesuati 780 ☎041 520 6466.
Tues-Sun 12.30-3pm & 6.30-10pm.
MAP PP.60-61, POCKET MAP E8

Stretching onto the waterfront
outside the *Calcina* hotel, to
which it's attached, this is one
of the most pleasant
restaurants in Dorsoduro. The
service is excellent, the food is
good (main courses cost in the
region of €20), and the view of
Giudecca from the terrace is
wonderful.

ONIGA

Campo S. Barnaba 2852 ☎041 522 4410. Mon
& Wed-Sun noon-3pm & 7-11pm. MAP
PP.60-61, POCKET MAP A15.

One of several good mid-range
restaurants in the San Barnaba
area, this place has received

LA PISCINA

some very good press in Italy,
though the food is dependable
rather than outstanding. The
tone of the place – youthful,
friendly and efficient – is
appealing, though, and the set
lunch, at around €20, is a very
good deal; in the evening there
is a choice of set meals
(costing €30), whch includes a
vegetarian option.

Bars and snacks

AI DO DRAGHI

Campo S. Margherita 3665. April-Oct
8am-2am; Nov-March 8am-11pm; closed
Thurs. MAP PP.60-61, POCKET MAP A14

Taking its name from the two
dragons on the wall opposite,
this is a tiny, friendly
café-bar, with a good range
of wines. Pop in to the back
room, which exhibits the
work of local photographers
and artists.

CAFÉ NOIR

Crosera 3805. Mon-Fri 11am-2am, Sat & Sun
7pm-2am. MAP PP.60-61, POCKET MAP B13

A favourite student bar serving
well-priced cocktails. There is
often live music here on
Tuesday nights.

CANTINA DEL VINO GIÀ SCHIAVI

Fondamenta Nani 992. Mon–Sat 8am–8pm, Sun 10am–1pm. MAP PP.60-61, POCKET MAP B16

Known to Venetians as the *Cantinone* or *Al Bottegon*, this is a great and long-established bar and wine shop, on the other side of the canal from San Trovaso church. Excellent *cicheti* and generously filled panini too.

DA CÒDROMA

Fondamenta Briati 2540. Mon–Sat 10am–4pm & 6–11pm, Sun noon–3.30pm. MAP PP.60-61, POCKET MAP C6

Perennially popular with Venice's students and with people of all ages from the surrounding parishes, this wood-panelled *osteria* has refectory style tables and serves simple meals, but most of the punters are just here for a glass, a snack and a chat. It hosts occasional poetry readings and live jazz as well.

IMPRONTA CAFÈ

Calle Crosera San Pantalon 3815 ☎ 041 275 0386, ⊕ improntacafevenice.com. Mon–Fri 7am–2am, Sat 8am–2am. MAP PP.60-61, POCKET MAP B13

CAFÈ NOIR

A very welcome addition to the Venetian scene, *Impronta Cafè* is a distinctively bright, stylish and youthful bar-café-restaurant that is busy at all hours of the day. Drop in for a quick morning coffee, come in to enjoy an evening spritz or even settle down with a nightcap, or sit down for a full meal – the menu changes daily, with mains costing €13–16.

MARGARET DUCHAMP

Campo S. Margherita 3019. Mon & Wed–Sun 9am–2am. MAP PP.60-61, POCKET MAP A14

Until *Orange* opened for business opposite, *Margaret DuChamp* was undisputedly this area's first-choice bar for style-conscious Venetians, and even with the competition across the street it's still kept its edge. It has ranks of seats out on the campo for much of the year.

OSTERIA ALLA BIFORA

Campo S. Margherita 2930. Mon–Sat noon–3pm & 7–11pm. MAP PP.60-61, POCKET MAP A14

With a candlelit, wood-beamed and brick interior, friendly service, good wine, excellent *cicheti*, and large plates of meat and cheese if you need more calories, the *Osteria Alla Bifora* is one of several fine places for a pit-stop on Campo di Santa Margherita.

VINUS VENEZIA

Calle del Scaleter 3961. Daily 11am–11pm. MAP PP.60-61, POCKET MAP B13

A bijou and very pleasant wine bar near San Rocco; the stock of wines here isn't huge, but you will find that the selection has certainly been chosen with care, and the panini are succulent.

San Polo and Santa Croce

The focal points of daily life in San Polo and Santa Croce are the sociable open space of Campo San Polo and the Rialto area, once the commercial heart of the Republic and still the home of a market that's famous far beyond the city's boundaries. The bustle of the stalls and the unspoilt bars are a good antidote to cultural overload. Nobody, however, should miss the extraordinary pair of buildings in the southern part of San Polo: the colossal Gothic church of the Frari and the Scuola Grande di San Rocco, decorated with an unforgettable cycle of paintings by Tintoretto. In the northern part of the district, Venice's modern art, oriental and natural history museums are clustered together on the bank of the Canal Grande: the first two collections occupy one of the city's most magnificent palaces. As ever, numerous treasures are also scattered among the minor churches, notably San Cassiano, San Giovanni Elemosinario and San Simeone Profeta.

THE RIALTO

MAP PP.76–77, POCKET MAP E11–F12

Relatively stable building land and a good defensive position drew some of the earliest lagoon settlers to the high bank (*rivo alto*) that was to develop into the Rialto district. As the political centre of Venice grew around San Marco, the Rialto became the commercial area. In the

SHOPS ON THE RIALTO BRIDGE

twelfth century Europe's first state bank was opened here, and the financiers of this quarter were to be the heavyweights of the international currency exchanges for the next three hundred years and more. And through the **markets of the Rialto** Venice earned a reputation as the bazaar of Europe. Trading had been going on here for over four hundred years when, in the winter of 1514, a fire destroyed everything in the area except the church. Reconstruction began almost straight away: the **Fabbriche Vecchie di Rialto** (the arcaded buildings along the Ruga degli Orefici and around the Campo San Giacomo) were finished eight years after the fire, with Sansovino's **Fabbriche Nuove di Rialto** (running along the Canal Grande) following about thirty years later.

RIALTO MARKET STALL

Today's Rialto market is tamer than that of Venice at its peak, but it's still one of the liveliest spots in the city, and one of the few places where it's possible to stand in a crowd and hear nothing but Italian spoken. You'll find fruit sellers, vegetable stalls, cheese kiosks, a number of good *alimentari* and some fine bars and *osterie* here. The Rialto market is open Monday to Saturday 8am to 1pm, with a few stalls opening again later in the afternoon; the **Pescheria** (fish market) is closed on Monday as well.

SAN GIACOMO DI RIALTO

MAP PP.76–77, POCKET MAP F12

Venetian legend asserts that the city was founded at noon on Friday, March 25, 421; from the same legend derives the claim that the church of San Giacomo di Rialto, or San Giacometto, was consecrated in that year,

and is thus the oldest church in Venice; it was, however, rebuilt in 1071. Parts of the present structure date from this period – the interior's six columns of ancient Greek marble have eleventh-century Veneto-Byzantine capitals – and it seems likely that the reconstruction of the church prompted the establishment of the market here. It's now used as a concert hall – mainly Vivaldi, of course.

IL GOBBO

MAP PP.76–77, POCKET MAP F12

On the opposite side of the campo from the church crouches a stone figure known as Il Gobbo di Rialto or the Rialto hunchback. It supports a granite platform from which state proclamations were read simultaneously with their announcement from the Pietra del Bando, beside San Marco; it had another role as well – certain wrongdoers were sentenced to run the gauntlet, stark naked, from the Piazza to the Gobbo.

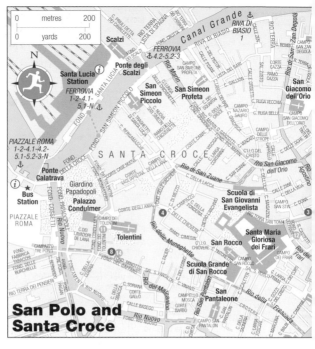

San Polo and Santa Croce

SAN GIOVANNI ELEMOSINARIO

Mon–Sat 10am–5pm. €3 or Chorus Pass.
MAP ABOVE, POCKET MAP E12

The church of San Giovanni
Elemosinario is so solidly
packed into the surrounding
buildings that its campanile is
the only conspicuous
indication of its presence.
Founded in the eleventh
century, it was wrecked in the
huge Rialto fire of 1514 – only
the campanile survived – and
rebuilt in 1527–29. Most of the
church's decoration dates from
the decades immediately
following the rebuild; the best
artworks are **Titian**'s high
altarpiece of *St John the
Almsgiver*, and **Pordenone**'s
nearby *SS Catherine, Sebastian
and Roch*. The frescoes in the
cupola, featuring a gang of
very chunky cherubs, are also
by Pordenone.

SAN CASSIANO

Daily 9am–noon & 5–7pm. MAP ABOVE,
POCKET MAP D11

The thirteenth-century
campanile is the only appealing
aspect of the exterior of the
church of San Cassiano, but
inside there are three fine
paintings by **Tintoretto**: *The
Resurrection*, *The Descent into
Limbo* and *The Crucifixion*. The
third is one of the most
startling pictures in Venice –
centred on the ladder on which
the executioners stand, it's
painted as though the observer
were lying in the grass at the
foot of the Cross.

Campo San Cassiano was
the site of the **first public
opera house** in the world – it
opened in 1636, at the peak of
Monteverdi's career. Long into
the following century Venice's
opera houses were among the

	SHOPS	
Francis Model	1
La Scialuppa	2

ACCOMMODATION	
Alex	6
Ca' Angeli	9
Ca' Arco Antico	7
Ca' Favretto-	
San Cassiano	2
Ca' San Giorgio	1
Domus Civica	4
Oltre il Giardino	3
Salieri	8
Sturion	5

RESTAURANTS	
Antiche	
Carampane	7
Antico Dolo	9
Bancogiro	6
Da Fiore	8
Muro Frari	13
Muro San Stae	1
Ribot	14
Vecio Fritolin	2

CAFÉS AND PASTICCERIE	
Caffè dei Frari	12
Caffè del Doge	10

BARS	
All'Arco	5
Al Mercà	4
Da Lele	11
Do Mori	3

most active in Europe; around five hundred works received their first performances here in the first half of the eighteenth century.

CAMPO SANTA MARIA MATER DOMINI

MAP ABOVE, POCKET MAP D11

The small Campo Santa Maria Mater Domini is a perfect Venetian miscellany, untouched by tourism – a thirteenth-century house (the Casa Zane), a few ramshackle Gothic houses, an assortment of stone reliefs of indeterminate age, a fourteenth-century wellhead in the centre, a workaday bar, a couple of shops, and a hairdresser's. The church of **Santa Maria Mater Domini** (Tues–Fri 10am–noon), a handsome early sixteenth-century building, boasts an endearing *Martyrdom of St Christina* by **Vincenzo Catena**, showing a flight of angels plucking the saint from a carpet-like Lago di Bolsena, into which she had been hurled with a millstone for an anchor.

RIALTO SHOPPING

CA' PÉSARO

capesaro.visitmuve.it. Tues–Sun: April–Oct 10am–6pm; Nov–March 10am–5pm. €10 or Museum Pass. MAP PP.76–77, POCKET MAP D10–11

The immense Ca' Pésaro was bequeathed to the city at the end of the nineteenth century by the Duchessa Felicità Bevilacqua La Masa who stipulated in her will that it should provide accommodation for impoverished young artists. Adventurous shows were staged here for a while, but instead of becoming a permanent centre for the living arts the palazzo has become home to the **Galleria Internazionale d'Arte Moderna**. The name is slightly misleading: a few of the foreign heavyweights of modern art are here (eg Klimt, Kandinsky, Matisse, Klee, Picasso, Ernst and Miró), but in essence this is a very selective overview of Italian art in the late nineteenth and twentieth centuries. The top-floor rooms are home to the **Museo Orientale**, a tightly packed array of porcelain, armour, musical instruments, clothing, and enough weaponry to equip a private army. Many of the pieces are exquisite – look out for an incredibly intricate chess set, and a room full of marvellous lacquerwork.

Who's San Stae?

Among the chief characteristics of the **Venetian vernacular** are its tendencies to slur consonants, abbreviate syllables and swallow vowels. For example, the Italian name Giuseppe here becomes Isepo, Giuliano becomes Zulian, Eustachio becomes Stae, Biagio becomes Biasio (or Blasio), Agostino shrinks to Stin, and Giovanni is Zuan or Zan – as in San Zan Degolà, for San Giovanni Decollato.

You'll also see *dose* instead of *doge*, *do* instead of *due*, *nove* instead of *nuove* and *fontego* for *fondaco*. And you may notice, too, that the letter "x" occasionally replaces "z" (as in v*enexiana*), and that the final vowel is habitually lopped off Venetian surnames, as in Giustinian, Loredan and Vendramin, to cite just three of the most conspicuous instances.

SAN STAE

Mon–Sat 10am–5pm. €3 or Chorus Pass.
MAP PP.76–77, POCKET MAP D10

Continuing along the line of the Canal Grande from the Ca' Pésaro, Calle Pésaro takes you over the Rio della Rioda, and so to the seventeenth-century church of San Stae. Its Baroque facade is enlivened by precarious statues, and the *marmorino* (pulverized marble) surfaces of the interior make San Stae as bright as an operating theatre on sunny days. In the chancel there's a series of paintings from the beginning of the eighteenth century, the pick of which are *The Martyrdom of St James the Great* by Piazzetta (low on the left), *The Liberation of St Peter* by Sebastiano Ricci (same row) and *The Martyrdom of St Bartholomew* by Giambattista Tiepolo (opposite). Exhibitions and concerts are often held in San Stae.

PALAZZO MOCENIGO

Ⓦ mocenigo.visitmuve.it. Tues–Sun: April–Oct 10am–5pm; Nov–March 10am–4pm. €8 or Museum Pass. MAP PP.76–77, POCKET MAP C11

Halfway down the alley flanking San Stae is the early seventeenth-century Palazzo Mocenigo, now home to a centre for the study of textiles and clothing. The library and archive of the study centre occupy part of the building, but a substantial portion of the *piano nobile* is open to the public, and there are few Venetian interiors of this date that have been so meticulously preserved: the rooms are full of portraits, antique furniture, Murano chandeliers and display cases of dandified clothing and cobweb-fine lacework. The curtains are kept closed to protect such delicate items as floral silk stockings, silvery padded waistcoats, and an extraordinarily embroidered outfit once worn by what must have been the best-dressed 5-year-old in town.

SAN GIOVANNI DECOLLATO

Mon–Sat 10am–noon. MAP PP.76–77, POCKET MAP C10

The signposted route to the train station passes the deconsecrated church of San Giovanni Decollato, or San Zan Degolà in dialect – it means "St John the Beheaded". Established in the opening years of the eleventh century, it has retained its layout through several alterations; the columns and capitals of the nave date from the first century of its existence, and parts of its fragmentary **frescoes** (at the east end) may be of the same age. Some of the paintings are certainly thirteenth century, and no other church in Venice has frescoes that predate them. The church also has one of the city's characteristic ship's-keel ceilings.

THE MUSEO STORICO NATURALE

Ⓦ msn.visitmuve.it. June–Oct Tues–Sun 10am–6pm; Nov–May Tues–Fri 9am–5pm, Sat & Sun 10am–6pm. €8 or Museum Pass. MAP PP.76–77, POCKET MAP C10

In 2012 the Museo di Storia Naturale, inside the Fondaco dei Turchi, reopened after lengthy restoration. The fossil collection is displayed with great imagination, and you'll also find an extraordinary miscellany of items gathered by Giovanni Miani during his 1859–60 expedition to trace the source of the Nile, a hideous array of hunting trophies, and an excellent reconstruction of a Wunderkammer or Cabinet of Curiosities. It's a huge and fascinating collection, but the captions are in Italian only.

SAN GIACOMO DELL'ORIO

Mon–Sat 10am–5pm. €3 or Chorus Pass.
MAP PP.76–77, POCKET MAP B11

Standing in a lovely campo which, despite its size, you could easily miss if you weren't looking for it, San Giacomo dell'Orio is an ancient and atmospheric church. Founded in the ninth century (the shape of the apse betrays its Byzantine origins), it was rebuilt in 1225 and remodelled on numerous subsequent occasions, notably when its **ship's-keel roof** was added in the fourteenth century. Several fine paintings are displayed here. The main altarpiece, *Madonna and Four Saints*, was painted by Lorenzo Lotto in 1546, shortly before he left the city complaining that the Venetians had not treated him fairly; the Crucifix that hangs in the air in front of it is attributed to Paolo Veneziano. In the left transept there's an altarpiece by Paolo Veronese, and there's a fine set of pictures from Veronese's workshop on the ceiling of the **new sacristy**. The **old sacristy** is a showcase for the art of Palma il Giovane, whose cycle in celebration of the Eucharist covers the walls and part of the ceiling.

SAN SIMEONE PROFETA

Mon–Sat 8am–noon & 5–6.30pm.
MAP PP.76–77, POCKET MAP A11

Originating in the tenth century, the church of San Simeone Profeta (or Grande) has often been rebuilt – most extensively in the eighteenth century, when the city sanitation experts, anxious about the condition of the plague victims who had been buried under the flagstones in the 1630 epidemic, ordered the whole floor to be relaid. Though undistinguished as a building, it's remarkable for its reclining **effigy of St Simeon** (to the left of the chancel), a luxuriantly bearded, larger than lifesize figure, whose half-open mouth disturbingly creates the impression of the moment of death. According to its inscription, it was sculpted in 1317 by **Marco Romano**, but some experts doubt that the sculpture can be that old, as nothing else of that date bears comparison with it.

CAMPO SAN POLO

MAP PP.76–77, POCKET MAP C12

South of the Rialto, **Ruga Vecchia San Giovanni** constitutes the first leg of the right bank's nearest equivalent to the Mercerie of San Marco, a reasonably straight chain of shop-lined alleyways that's interrupted by Campo San Polo, the largest square in Venice after the Piazza. In earlier times it was the site of weekly markets and occasional fairs, as well as being used as a parade ground and bullfighting arena. And on one occasion Campo San Polo was the scene of a bloody act of political retribution: on February 26, 1548, Lorenzaccio de'Medici, having fled Florence after murdering the deranged duke Alessandro (a distant relative and former friend), was murdered here by assassins sent by Duke Cosimo I, Alessandro's successor.

SAN POLO

Mon–Sat 10am–5pm.€3 or Chorus Pass. MAP PP.76–77, POCKET MAP C13

The bleak interior of San Polo church is worth a visit for a *Last Supper* by Tintoretto (on the left as you enter) and a cycle of the *Stations of the Cross* (*Via Crucis*) by Giandomenico Tiepolo in the Oratory of the Crucifix (entrance under organ). This powerful series, painted when the artist was only 20, appears less frivolous than Giandomenico customarily is, even if some of the scenes do feature lustrously attired sophisticates who seem to have drifted in from the salons of eighteenth-century Venice. A couple of Tiepolo ceiling panels and two other easel paintings supplement the *Via Crucis*; back in the main part of the church, paintings by Giando-

menico's father and Veronese are displayed on the second altar opposite the door and in the chapel on the left of the chancel respectively, but neither shows the artist at his best.

CASA GOLDONI

Calle dei Nomboli 2794 ⓦ carlogoldoni. visitmuve.it.. Daily except Wed: April–Oct 10am–5pm; Nov–March 10am–4pm. €5 or Museum Pass. MAP PP.76–77, POCKET MAP C13

The fifteenth-century **Palazzo Centani** was the birthplace of **Carlo Goldoni** (1707–93), the playwright who transformed the *commedia dell'arte* from a vehicle for semi-improvised clowning into a medium for sharp political observation. Goldoni's plays are still the staple of theatrical life in Venice, and there's no risk of running out of material – allegedly, he once bet a friend that he could produce one play a week for a whole year, and won. Goldoni's home now houses a theatre studies institute and the **Museo Goldoni**, a very small collection of first editions, portraits and theatrical paraphernalia, including some eighteenth-century marionettes and a miniature theatre.

SANTA MARIA GLORIOSA DEI FRARI

Mon–Sat 9am–6pm, Sun 1–6pm. €3 or Chorus Pass. MAP PP76–77, POCKET MAP B13

Santa Maria Gloriosa dei Frari – always abbreviated to the **Frari** – was founded by the Franciscans around 1250, not long after the death of their founder, but almost no sooner was the first church completed (in 1338) than work began on a vast replacement, a project which took well over a hundred years. The campanile, one of the city's landmarks and the tallest after San Marco's, was finished in 1396.

You're unlikely to fall in love at first sight with this mountain of brick, but the outside of the church is a misleadingly dull prelude to an astounding interior. Apart from the Accademia and the Salute, the Frari is the only building in Venice with more than a single first-rate work by **Titian**, and one of these – the **Assumption** – you'll see right away, as it soars over the high altar. It's a piece of compositional and colouristic bravura for which there was no

precedent in Venetian art (no previous altarpiece had so emphasized the vertical axis), and the other Titian masterpiece here, the **Madonna di Ca'Pésaro** (on the left wall, between the third and fourth columns), was equally innovative in its displacement of the figure of the Virgin from the centre of the picture. Other paintings to look out for are Bartolomeo Vivarini's *St Mark Enthroned* (in the Cappella Corner, at the end of the left transept); Alvise Vivarini's *St Ambrose and other Saints* (in the adjoining chapel, where you'll also find the grave of Monteverdi); and, above all, **Giovanni Bellini**'s serene and solemn *Madonna and Child with SS. Nicholas of Bari, Peter, Mark and Benedict*, in the **sacristy**.

Apart from its paintings, the Frari is also remarkable for **Donatello**'s luridly naturalistic wooden statue *St John the Baptist* (in the chapel to the right of the transept), the beautiful fifteenth-century monks' choir, and its wealth of extravagant tombs. Two of the finest monuments flank the Titian *Assumption*: on the left is the proto-Renaissance **tomb of Doge Niccolò Tron**, by Antonio Rizzo and assistants (1476); on the right, the more archaic and chaotic **tomb of Doge Francesco Fóscari**, carved shortly after Fóscari's death in 1457 (after 34 years as doge) by Antonio and Paolo Bregno.

Against the right-hand wall of the nave stands the house-sized **monument to Titian**, built in the mid-nineteenth century on the supposed place of his burial. The artist died in 1576, in around his ninetieth year, a casualty of the plague; such was the esteem in which Titian was held, he was the only victim to be allowed a church burial in the course of the outbreak. The marble pyramid on the opposite side of the church is the **Mausoleum of Canova**, erected by pupils of the sculptor, following a design he himself had made for the tombs of Titian and Maria Christina of Austria. Finally, you can't fail to notice what is surely the most grotesque monument in the city, the tomb of **Doge Giovanni Pésaro** (1669), held aloft by gigantic ragged-trousered Moors and decomposing corpses.

THE SCUOLA GRANDE DI SAN ROCCO

ⓦ scuolagrandesanrocco.it. Daily 9.30am– 5.30pm. €10. MAP PP76–77, POCKET MAP B13

Unless you've been to the Scuola Grande di San Rocco you can't properly appreciate the genius of Tintoretto. Ruskin called it "one of the three most precious buildings in Italy", and it's not difficult to understand why he resorted to such hyperbole. (His other votes were for the Sistine Chapel and the Camposanto at Pisa; the

latter was badly damaged in World War II.) The unremitting concentration and restlessness of Tintoretto's paintings won't inspire unqualified enthusiasm in everyone, but even those who prefer their art at a lower voltage should find this an astounding experience.

From its foundation in 1478, the special concern of this particular *scuola* was the relief of the sick – a continuation of the Christian mission of its patron saint, St Roch (Rocco) of Montpellier, who in 1315 left his home town to work among plague victims in Italy. The Scuola had been going for seven years when the body of the saint was brought to Venice from Germany, and the consequent boom in donations was so great that in 1489 it acquired the status of *scuola grande*. In 1527 the city was hit by an outbreak of plague, and the Scuola's revenue rocketed to record levels as gifts poured in from people hoping to secure St Roch's protection against the disease. The fattened coffers paid for this building, and for **Tintoretto**'s amazing cycle of more than fifty major paintings.

The narrative sequence begins with the first picture in the lower room – the *Annunciation*. But to appreciate Tintoretto's development you have to begin in the smaller room on the upper storey – the **Sala dell'Albergo**. This is dominated by the stupendous *Crucifixion* (1565), the most compendious image of the event ever painted. Tintoretto's other works here – aside from the *Glorification of St Roch* in the middle of the ceiling (the piece that won him the contract to decorate the whole room) – are on the entrance wall.

Tintoretto finished his contribution to the Sala dell'Albergo in 1567. Eight years later, when the Scuola decided to proceed with the embellishment of the main upper hall – the **chapter house** – he undertook to do the work

in return for nothing more than his expenses. In the event he was awarded a lifetime annuity, and then commenced the **ceiling**. The Scuola's governors were so pleased with these three large panels that he was given the task of decorating the entire interior – a feat of sustained inventiveness that has few equals in Western art. Though he was in his late sixties when he came to paint the **lower hall**, there is no sign of flagging creativity: indeed, the landscapes in *The Flight into Egypt* and the meditative depictions of *St Mary Magdalen* and *St Mary of Egypt* are among the finest he ever created.

THE CHURCH OF SAN ROCCO

Daily 9.30am–5.30pm. MAP PP.76–77, POCKET MAP B13

Before or after a visit to the neighbouring Scuola of San Rocco, pop into the church of San Rocco, where – on the right wall of the nave – you'll find *St Roch Taken to Prison*, and below it *The Pool of Bethesda*; the latter is definitely by Tintoretto, the former possibly by him. Between the altars on the other side are a couple of good pictures by **Pordenone** – *St Christopher* and *St Martin*. Four large paintings by Tintoretto hang in the chancel, often either lost in the gloom or glazed with sunlight: the best (both painted in 1549) are *St Roch Curing the Plague Victims* (lower right) and *St Roch in Prison* (lower left).

THE SCUOLA DI SAN GIOVANNI EVANGELISTA

ⓦ www.scuolasangiovanni.it. MAP PP.76–77, POCKET MAP B12

The Scuola di San Giovanni Evangelista, which nestles in a

THE CHURCH OF SAN ROCCO

line of drab buildings near to the Frari, was founded in 1261 and its finest hour came in 1369 when it was presented with a relic of the True Cross. The miracles effected by the relic were commemorated in a series of paintings by Carpaccio, Gentile Bellini and others, now in the Accademia. The interior is sporadically open to the public (visiting hours are posted monthly on the website), but the chief attraction of the Scuola is the superb screen of the outer courtyard; built in 1481 by Pietro Lombardo, it's a wonderfully delicate piece of marble carving.

THE TOLENTINI

Daily 8am–noon & 4–7pm. MAP PP.76–77, POCKET MAP C5

The portentous church of San Nicolò da Tolentino – alias dei Tolentini – was the Venetian home of the Theatine Order, which found refuge in Venice after the Sack of Rome by the army of Charles V in 1527. It was begun in 1590 by Palladio's follower Scamozzi, and finished in 1714 by the addition of a freestanding portico – the first in Venice – designed by Andrea Tirali.

Among scores of seventeenth-century paintings here, two stand out. The first is a *St Jerome* by Johann Lys, at the foot of the chancel steps, on the left; it was painted in 1628, just two years before German-born Lys died of the plague, aged 33. The other is *St Lawrence Giving Alms* by Bernardo Strozzi, round the corner from the Lys painting, to the left. Up the left wall of the chancel swirls the best Baroque monument in Venice: the **tomb of Francesco Morosini**, the Patriach of Venice, created in 1678 by a Genoese sculptor, Filippo Parodi.

THE GIARDINO PAPADOPOLI

MAP PP.76–77, POCKET MAP C4–5

If fatigue is setting in and you need a pit-stop, make for the nearby Giardino Papadopoli, which is just over the Rio dei Tolentini. Formerly one of Venice's biggest private gardens, it is now owned by the city.

Shops

FRANCIS MODEL

Ruga Vecchia San Giovanni 773a. Mon–Sat
10am–7pm, Sun 10.30am–6pm. MAP PP.76–77,
POCKET MAP E12

This father-and-son workshop
produces high-quality
handbags and briefcases.

LA SCIALUPPA

Calle Seconda Saoneri 2681 🕸 veniceboats
.com. Mon–Sat 9.30am–12.30pm & 3–6pm.
MAP PP.76–77, POCKET MAP C13

For a uniquely Venetian gift, call
in at Gilberto Penzo's shop,
which sells models, model kits
and elegantly drawn plans of
Venetian boats.

Cafés

CAFFÈ DEI FRARI

Fondamenta dei Frari 2564. Mon–Sat
8am–9pm. MAP PP.76–77, POCKET MAP B13

Very atmospheric and pretty
Belle Époque-styled bar-café
opposite the Frari's front door.

CAFFÈ DEL DOGE

Calle dei Cinque 609 🕸 caffedeldoge.com.
Mon–Sat 8.30am–8pm, Sun 9am–1pm. MAP
PP.76–77, POCKET MAP E12

Fantastically good coffee, served
in a chic minimalist set-up very
close to the Rialto Bridge.

Restaurants

ANTICHE CARAMPANE

Rio Terrà delle Carampane 1911 ☎ 041 524
0165, 🕸 antichecarampane.com. Tues–Sat
12.30–2.30pm & 7.30–10.30pm. MAP PP.76–77,
POCKET MAP D12

If not the most tourist-friendly
place in the city (a semi-jokey
notice that tells you there's "No
lasagne, no pizza, no menu
turistico"), the *Carampane* is a
thoroughbred Venetian trattoria,
serving excellent seafood in a

ANTICO DOLO

cosy interior – with outside
seating in fine weather. The brief
menu is often wholly fish-based;
three courses cost around €60.

ANTICO DOLO

Ruga Vecchia San Giovanni 778 ☎ 041 522
6546, 🕸 www.anticodolo.it. Daily noon–10pm.
MAP PP.76–77, POCKET MAP E12

You can pop into this excellent,
long-established *osteria* for a
few *cicheti* and a glass of Merlot
and come away just a few euros
poorer; or you can take a table
and eat an excellent meal for
something in the region of €40.

BANCOGIRO

Sottoportego del Banco Giro 122. Tues–Sun
11am–midnight. MAP PP.76–77, POCKET MAP F12

Very popular *osteria*, in a
splendid location in the midst
of the Rialto market. Come
here to nurse a glass of fine
wine beside the Canal Grande,
or nip upstairs to the dining
room for a not inexpensive but
well-prepared meal.

DA FIORE

Calle del Scaleter 2202a ☎ 041 731 308,
🕸 dafiore.net. Closed Sun & Mon. MAP
PP.76–77, POCKET MAP C12

Hyper-refined *Da Fiore* is
possibly the most famous

restaurant in Venice, and is certainly one of the most lauded, both by Italians and foreign foodies. It's amazingly expensive: the tasting menu is €120–140 per person, and you'll be paying €40–50 for your main course à la carte. If you're going to treat yourself here, make sure you get one of the two canalside tables on the tiny terrace.

MURO SAN STAE

Campiello del Spezier 2048–50 ☎ 041 524 1628. San Stae branch daily noon–3pm & 6–11pm; Frari branch daily 11am–1am. MAP PP.76–77. POCKET MAP C11 & C13

Muro offers a good range of pizzas plus an imaginative seafood menu on which main courses cost about €15. The styling is spartan, the service excellent and there is seating outside. *Muro Frari*, at Rio Terrà dei Frari 2604, has the same menu and style.

RIBOT

Fondamenta Minotto 158 ☎ 041 524 2486, ⓦ ristoranteribot.com. Mon–Sat 12.30–2.30pm & 7–10.30pm. MAP PP.76–77. POCKET MAP G4

Named after a famous racehorse (in case you're wondering about the logo), *Ribot* is an old-fashioned, good-value restaurant, with a menu that draws on recipes from beyond the Veneto, and has a lovely garden out back. Main courses are mostly under €20, and there are some well-priced set menus.

VECIO FRITOLIN

Calle della Regina 2262 ☎ 041 522 2881, ⓦ veciofritolin.it. Tues noon–2.30pm, Wed–Sun noon–2.30pm & 7–10.30pm. MAP PP.76–77. POCKET MAP D11

The name translates as "the old frying-place", and one of its signature dishes is a succulent fry-up of estuary fish, but the *Vecio Fritolin* has come a long way since its time as a purveyor of Venetian fast food. Now you'll find seafood making imaginative use of local and seasonal produce. A friendly and well-reputed spot that attracts plenty of locals. You'll pay upward of €60 per person.

Bars and snacks

ALL'ARCO

Calle dell'Ochialer 436. Mon–Sat 7am–5pm. MAP PP.76–77. POCKET MAP E12

A great stand-up Rialto bar, tucked under the end of the sottoportego opposite S. Giovanni Elemosinario; does superb *sarde in saor* and other snacks.

AL MERCÀ

Campo Cesare Battisti 213. Mon–Sat 7am–3pm & 6–9pm. MAP PP.76–77. POCKET MAP E12

This minuscule stand-up Rialto bar is perfect for a quick *panino* and prosecco.

DA LELE

Campo dei Tolentini 183. Mon–Fri 6am–8pm, Sat 6am–2pm. MAP PP.76–77. POCKET MAP C5

As you can tell by the opening hours, this tiny and utterly authentic stand-up bar attracts a lot of custom from workers en route to or from Piazzale Roma. Sandwiches and rolls made freshly to order; wine by the glass from just 60c.

DO MORI

Calle Do Mori 429. Mon–Sat 8am–7.30pm. MAP PP.76–77. POCKET MAP E12

Hidden just off Ruga Vecchia S. Giovanni, *Do Mori* is one of the city's most authentic old-style Venetian bars. It's a single narrow room, with no seating, packed every evening with shopworkers, Rialto porters and locals just out for a stroll. Delicious snacks, good range of wines, terrific atmosphere.

Cannaregio

Don't be put off by the hustle around the train station – in Cannaregio, Venice's northernmost section, it's very easy to get well away from the tourist crowds as you explore the area's enticing backwaters. The pleasures of this *sestiere* are generally more a matter of atmosphere than of specific sights, but you shouldn't leave Venice without seeing the Ghetto, the first area in the world to bear that name and one of Venice's most evocative quarters. There are some special buildings to visit too: Madonna dell'Orto, with its astonishing Tintoretto paintings; Sant'Alvise and the Palazzo Labia, both remarkable for works by Giambattista Tiepolo; the Ca' d'Oro, a gorgeous Canal Grande palace housing a sizeable art collection; the highly photogenic Santa Maria dei Miracoli; and the Gesuiti, a Baroque creation which boasts perhaps the weirdest interior in the city.

THE SCALZI

Daily 7–11.50am & 4–6.50pm. MAP BELOW, POCKET MAP C3

Right by the station stands the Scalzi (formally Santa Maria di Nazaretta), which was begun in 1672 for the barefoot ("scalzi") order of Carmelites, but is anything but barefoot itself – the opulent interior is plated with dark, multicoloured marble and overgrown with Baroque statuary. Before an Austrian bomb plummeted through the roof in 1915 there was a great **Giambattista Tiepolo** ceiling here; a few scraps are preserved in the Accademia, and some wan frescoes by Tiepolo survive in the first chapel on the left and the second on the right. The second chapel on the left is the resting place of **Lodovico Manin** (d.1802), Venice's last doge.

SAN GEREMIA

Mon–Sat 8am–noon & 3.30–6.30pm, Sun 9.15am–12.15pm & 5.30–6.30pm. MAP BELOW, POCKET MAP D3

The church of San Geremia is where the travels of **St Lucy** eventually terminated – martyred in Syracuse in 304, she was stolen from Constantinople by Venetian Crusaders in 1204, then ousted from her own church in Venice in the mid-nineteenth century, when it was demolished to make way for the train station. Her desiccated body, wearing a lustrous silver mask, lies behind the altar, reclining above a donations box that bears the prayer "Saint Lucy, protect my eyes" – she's the patron saint of eyesight (and artists). Nothing else about the church is of interest, except the twelfth-century **campanile**, one of the oldest left in the city.

PALAZZO LABIA

☎ 041 524 2812 or check at the tourist office. Free. MAP PP.88–89, POCKET MAP D3

The Palazzo Labia, next door to San Geremia, was built in 1720–50 for a famously extravagant Catalan family by the name of Lasbias. No sooner was the interior completed than **Giambattista Tiepolo** was hired to cover the walls of the ballroom with **frescoes** depicting the story of Anthony and Cleopatra. RAI, the Italian state broadcasting company, now owns the palace, but they sometimes allow visitors in for a few hours each week.

SAN GIOBBE

Mon–Sat 10am–1.30pm. €3 or Chorus Pass. MAP PP.88–89, POCKET MAP C2

The Palazzo Labia's longest facade overlooks the **Canale di Cannaregio**, the main entrance to Venice before the rail and road links were constructed; if you turn left immediately before or after the Ponte delle Guglie, you'll reach the Ponte dei Tre Archi (Venice's only multiple-span bridge), where a left turn takes you to the church of San Giobbe. Dedicated to Job, whose

sufferings greatly endeared him to the Venetians (who were regularly afflicted with malaria, plague and a plethora of water-related diseases), the church is interesting mainly for its exquisitely carved doorway and chancel – the first Venetian projects of **Pietro Lombardo**. The best paintings – a fine triptych by Antonio Vivarini and a *Marriage of St Catherine* attributed to Andrea Previtali – are in the **sacristy**, along with a fifteenth-century terracotta bust of the great preacher St Bernardine, who in 1443 was a guest here (in what turned out to be the last year of his life) and whose canonization in 1450 was marked by the rebuilding of this church.

THE GHETTO

MAP PP.88–89, POCKET MAP D2

The name of the Venetian Ghetto – a name bequeathed to all other such enclaves of oppression – is probably derived from the Venetian dialect *geto*, foundry, which is what this area used to be. The creation of the Ghetto was a consequence of the War of the League of Cambrai, when hundreds of Jews fled the mainland in fear of the Imperial army. Gaining safe haven in Venice, many of the fugitives donated funds for the defence of the city, and were rewarded with permanent protection – at a price. In 1516 the **Ghetto Nuovo** became Venice's Jewish quarter, when all the city's Jews were forced to move here. At night the Ghetto was sealed by gates, yet Venice was markedly liberal by the standards of the time, and the Ghetto's population was often swelled by refugees from less tolerant societies – indeed, the Jewish population soon spread into the **Ghetto Vecchio** and the **Ghetto Nuovissimo**. The gates of the Ghetto were finally torn down by Napoleon in 1797, but it wasn't until the unification of Italy that Jews achieved equal status with their fellow citizens.

Each wave of Jewish immigrants maintained their own synagogues with their distinctive rites: the **Scola Tedesca** (for German Jews) was founded in 1528, the **Scola al Canton** (probably Jews from Provence) in 1531–32, the **Scola Levantina** (eastern Mediterranean) in 1538, the **Scola Spagnola** (Spanish) at an uncertain date in the later sixteenth century, and the **Scola Italiana** in 1575. Funded by particularly

prosperous trading communities, the Scola Levantina and the Scola Spagnola are the most lavish of the synagogues, and are the only two still used on a daily basis.

Depending on the season, one of these can be viewed, along with the Scola al Canton and the Scola Italiana, in an informative English-language guided tour that begins in the **Museo Ebraico**, above the Scola Tedesca (daily except Sat and Jewish hols: June–Sept 10am–7pm; Oct–May 10am–5.30pm; €4 or free with tour, which costs €10; tours in English on the half-hour, last tour June–Sept 5.30pm, Oct–May 4.30pm). The museum's collection consists mainly of silverware, sacred objects, textiles and furniture.

CAMPO GHETTO NUOVO

PRESENTATION OF THE VIRGIN BY TINTORETTO, MADONNA DELL'ORTO

SANT'ALVISE

Mon–Sat 1.45–5pm. €3 or Chorus Pass. MAP PP.88–89, POCKET MAP E1

Located on the northern periphery of the city, the church of Sant'Alvise is notoriously prone to damp, but restoration has refreshed the chancel's immense *Road to Calvary* by Giambattista Tiepolo. His *Crown of Thorns* and *Flagellation*, slightly earlier works, hang on the right-hand wall of the nave. Under the nuns' choir you'll find eight small paintings, known as "The Baby Carpaccios" since Ruskin assigned them to the painter's precocious childhood; they're not actually by Carpaccio, but they were produced around 1470, when he would indeed have been just an infant. The extraordinary seventeenth-century trompe l'oeil ceiling is a collaboration between Antonio Torri and Paolo Ricchi. "Alvise", by the way, is the Venetian version of Luigi – the church is dedicated to St Louis of Toulouse.

MADONNA DELL'ORTO

Mon–Sat 10am–5pm. €2.50. MAP PP.88–89, POCKET MAP F1–2

Madonna dell'Orto, the Tintoretto family's parish church, is arguably the finest Gothic church in Venice. Founded in the name of Saint Christopher some time around 1350, it was popularly renamed after a large stone *Madonna* by **Giovanni de'Santi**, found in a nearby vegetable garden (*orto*), began working miracles; brought into the church in 1377, the heavily restored figure now sits in the Cappella di San Mauro (at the end of the right aisle).

Outside, the church is notable for its statue of St Christopher, its elegant portal and its **campanile**, one of the most notable landmarks when approaching Venice from the northern lagoon. Inside, paintings by **Tintoretto** make a massive impact, none more so than the epic pictures on each side of the choir: *The Last Judgement* and *The Making of* *the Golden Calf*. Other Tintorettos adorn the chancel, but best of all is the tender *Presentation of the Virgin*, at the end of the right aisle, which makes a fascinating comparison with Titian's Accademia version of the incident. A major figure of the early Venetian Renaissance – **Cima da Conegliano** – is represented by a *St John the Baptist and Other Saints*, on the first altar on the right; a *Madonna and Child* by Cima's great contemporary, Giovanni Bellini, used to occupy the first chapel on the left, but thieves made off with it in 1993.

Tintoretto spent the last two decades of his life in a house close to **Campo dei Mori**, to the south of the church. Four thirteenth-century statues stand around the campo: aggrieved citizens used to leave denunciations at the feet of "Sior Antonio Rioba" (the statue with the rusty nose), and circulate vindictive verses signed with his name.

STRADA NOVA

MAP PP.88–89, POCKET MAP D10–F11

The main land route between the train station and the Rialto Bridge was created in the 1870s by the Austrians. But whereas the Lista di Spagna and Rio Terrà San Leonardo were formed by filling canals with earth, the Strada Nova was created by simply ploughing a line straight through the houses that used to stand here. Outside the church of **Santa Fosca**, at the start of Strada Nova, stands a statue of a true Venetian hero, **Fra' Paolo Sarpi**. A brilliant scholar and scientist (he assisted Galileo), Sarpi was the adviser to the Venetian state in its row with the Vatican at the start of the seventeenth century, when the whole city was excommunicated for its refusal to accept papal jurisdiction in secular affairs. One night Sarpi was walking home past Santa Fosca when he was set upon by three men and left for dead with a dagger in his face. "I recognize the style of the Holy See", Sarpi quipped, punning on the word "stiletto". He survived.

Across the Strada Nova, the **Farmacia Ponci** has the oldest surviving shop interior in Venice, a wonderful display of seventeenth-century woodwork in walnut, with eighteenth-century majolica vases.

STRADA NOVA

CA' D'ORO

Calle Ca' d'Oro 3932 ⓦ cadoro.org. Mon
8.15am–2pm, Tues–Sat 8.15am–7.15pm, Sun
10am–6pm. €6. MAP PP.88–89, POCKET MAP E10–11

An inconspicuous calle leads
down to the Ca' d'Oro (House
of Gold), the finest example of
domestic Gothic architecture in
Venice. Built for procurator
Marino Contarini between
1425 and 1440, the palace takes
its name from its Canal Grande
facade: incorporating parts of
the thirteenth-century palace
that used to stand here, it was
highlighted in gold leaf,
ultramarine and vermilion –
materials which, as the three
most expensive pigments of the
day, spectacularly publicized
the wealth of its owner. The
house's cosmetics have now
worn off, but the facade has at
least survived unaltered.

Nowadays it's the home
of the **Galleria Giorgio
Franchetti**, a collection whose
main attraction is undoubtedly
the *St Sebastian* painted by
Mantegna shortly before his
death in 1506 – it's installed in
a chapel-like alcove on the first
floor. Many of the big names of
Venetian art are found on the
second floor, but the canvases
by Titian and Tintoretto are
not among their best, and
Pordenone's fragmentary
frescoes from Santo Stefano
require a considerable feat of
imaginative reconstruction, as
do the remains of Giorgione
and Titian's work from the
Fondaco dei Tedeschi (see
p.79). The Ca' d'Oro's
collection of sculpture, though
far less extensive than the array
of paintings, has more
outstanding items, notably
Tullio Lombardo's beautifully
carved *Young Couple*, and
superb portrait busts by
Bernini and Alessandro
Vittoria. Also arresting are a
sixteenth-century English
alabaster polyptych of *Scenes
from the Life of St Catherine*
and a case of Renaissance
medals that includes fine
specimens by **Gentile Bellini**
and **Pisanello**.

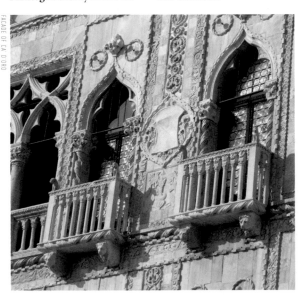

FACADE OF CA' D'ORO

SANTI APOSTOLI

Daily 7.30–11.30am & 5–7pm. MAP PP.88–89. POCKET MAP F11

At the eastern end of the Strada you come to the Campo dei Santi Apostoli, an elbow on the road from the Rialto to the train station. The most interesting part of Santi Apostoli church is the **Cappella Corner**, off the right side, where the altarpiece is the *Communion of St Lucy* by Giambattista Tiepolo. One of the inscriptions in the chapel is to Caterina Cornaro, who was buried here before being moved to San Salvatore; the tomb of her father Marco (on the right) is probably by Tullio Lombardo, who also carved the peculiar plaque of St Sebastian in the chapel to the right of the chancel.

SAN GIOVANNI CRISOSTOMO

Mon–Sat 8.30am–noon & 3.30–7pm, Sun 3.30–7pm. MAP PP.88–89, POCKET MAP F11

Tucked into the southernmost corner of Cannaregio stands San Giovanni Crisostomo (John the Golden-Mouthed), named after the famously eloquent Archbishop of Constantinople. An intimate church with a compact Greek-cross plan, it was possibly the last project of Mauro Codussi, and was built between 1497 and 1504.

It possesses two outstanding altarpieces: in the chapel to the right hangs one of the last works by **Giovanni Bellini**, *SS Jerome, Christopher and Louis of Toulouse*, painted in 1513 when the artist was in his eighties; and on the high altar, **Sebastiano del Piombo**'s *St John Chrysostom with SS John the Baptist, Liberale, Mary Magdalen, Agnes and Catherine*, painted in 1509–11.

SAN GIOVANNI CRISOSTOMO

TEATRO MALIBRAN

MAP PP.88–89, POCKET MAP G11–12

Behind San Giovanni Crisostomo stands the Teatro Malibran, which opened in the seventeenth century, was rebuilt in the 1790s, and soon after renamed in honour of the great soprano **Maria Malibran** (1808–36), who saved the theatre from bankruptcy by giving a fund-raising recital here. Quite recently unveiled following restoration, the Malibran is one of the city's chief venues for classical music. The Byzantine arches on the facade of the theatre are said to have once been part of the house of **Marco Polo**'s family, who probably lived in the place overlooking the canal at the back of the Malibran, visible from the Ponte Marco Polo. Polo's tales of his experiences in the empire of Kublai Khan were treated with incredulity when he returned to Venice in 1295. His habit of talking in superlatives earned him the nickname *Il Milione* (The Million). The nickname is preserved by the adjoining **Corte Prima del Milion** and **Corte Seconda del Milion**.

SANTA MARIA DEI MIRACOLI

Mon–Sat 10am–5pm. €3 or Chorus Pass.
MAP PP.88–89, POCKET MAP G11

A hop north of the Teatro Malibran stands the marble-clad church of Santa Maria dei Miracoli, usually known simply by the last word of its name. It was built in 1481–89 to house an image of the Madonna that was credited with the revival of a man who'd spent half an hour at the bottom of the Giudecca canal, and of a woman left for dead after being stabbed. Financed by gifts left at the painting's nearby shrine, the church was most likely designed by **Pietro Lombardo**; certainly he and his two sons Tullio and Antonio oversaw the construction, and the three of them executed much of the exquisite carving both inside and out.

The marble-lined **interior** contains some of the most intricate decorative sculpture to be seen in Venice. The *Annunciation* and half-length figures of two saints on the balustrade at the altar end are thought to be by Tullio; nobody is sure which members of the family created the rest of the carvings in this part of the church, though it's likely that Antonio was responsible for the children's heads at the base of the chancel arch and the adjacent siren figures. At the opposite end of the church, the columns below the nuns' choir are covered with extraordinary filigree stonework, featuring tiny birds with legs as thin as cocktail sticks. The miracle-working Madonna still occupies the altar, while overhead a sequence of fifty saints and prophets, painted in 1528 by Pier Pennacchi, is set into the Miracoli's unusual panelled ceiling.

THE GESUITI

Daily 10am–noon & 4–6pm. MAP PP.88–89, POCKET MAP G3–H3

The major monument in the northeastern corner of Cannaregio is **Santa Maria Assunta**, commonly known simply as the Gesuiti. Built for the Jesuits in 1714–29, six decades after the foundation here of their first monastery in Venice, the church was clearly planned to make an impression on a city that was habitually mistrustful of the order's close relationship with the papacy. Although the disproportionately huge facade clearly wasn't the work of a weekend, most of the effort went into the stupefying **interior**, where green and white marble covers every wall and stone is carved to resemble swags of damask. The only painting to seek out is the *Martyrdom of St Lawrence* on the first altar on the left, which was painted by **Titian** in 1558.

ORATORIO DEI CROCIFERI

MAP PP.88–89, POCKET MAP G3

Almost opposite the Gesuiti is the Oratorio dei Crociferi, the remnant of a convent complex founded in the twelfth century by the crusading religious order known as the Crociferi or the Bearers of the Cross. Part of the complex was given over to a hospice for poor women. (By the late sixteenth century Venice had around one hundred such institutions for the penniless.) In return for free meals and accommodation, these women were required to help in the maintenance of the convent and to pray each morning in the oratory, which in the 1580s was decorated by **Palma il Giovane** with a cycle of *Scenes from the History of the Order of the Crociferi*. Restored in the 1980s, the paintings show Palma's technique at its subtlest, and the richness of the colours is a good advertisement for modern cleaning techniques. Finding staff for the oratory is a perpetual problem, and at the moment the only way to get inside is to book a private visit – details on ⓦscalabovolo.org.

FONDAMENTE NOVE

MAP PP.88–89, POCKET MAP G2–J4

The long waterfront to the north of the Gesuiti, Fondamente Nove (or Nuove), is the chief departure point for **vaporetti** to San Michele, Murano and the northern lagoon. On a clear day you can follow their course as far as the distant island of Burano, with the startling sight of the snowy Dolomite peaks on the horizon.

Being relatively new, you'll find that this waterfront isn't solidly lined with historic buildings like its counterparts in the south of the city, the Zattere and the Riva degli Schiavone. The one house of interest along this stretch is the **Palazzo Donà delle Rose** on the corner of the Rio dei Gesuiti. Architecturally the palace is an oddity, as the main axis of its interior runs parallel to the water instead of at ninety degrees; the cornerstone was laid in 1610 by Doge Leonardo Donà, who died two years later from apoplexy after an argument with his brother about the layout of the house.

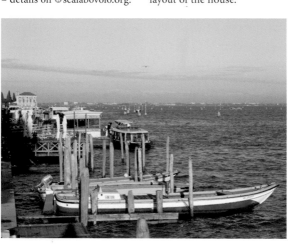

VIEW FROM THE FONDAMENTE NOVE

Shops

COIN

Salizzada S. Giovanni Crisostomo 5787 ☎ 041 520 3581, ⓦ coin.it. Mon–Sat 9.30am–7.30pm, Sun 11am–7.30pm. MAP PP.88–89. POCKET MAP F12.

There are branches of the Coin clothing department store all over Italy; this branch, near the church of San Giovanni Crisostomo, is the original.

MORI & BOZZI

Rio Terrà della Maddalena 2367. Mon–Sat 9.30am–7.30pm, plus Sun 11am–7pm in April, May, Sept & Oct. MAP PP.88–89, POCKET MAP E3

Stylish women's footwear from a range of small labels – no big names, but cool designs at moderate prices.

Restaurants

AI PROMESSI SPOSI

Calle dell'Oca 4367 ☎ 041 241 2747. Tues & Thurs–Sun 11.30am–2.15pm & 6–11pm, Wed 6–11pm only. MAP PP.88–89. POCKET MAP F11

Now run by former employees of *Alla Vedova* (see below), this moderately priced (mains around €15) and cosy little *osteria* specializes in *baccalà* and other traditional fish recipes. Excellent range of *cicheti* at the bar.

ALLA FONTANA

Fondamenta di Cannaregio 1102 ☎ 041 715 077. Tues–Sun 6.30–10pm. MAP PP.88–89, POCKET MAP D2

Once primarily a bar, *Alla Fontana* has transformed itself into an extremely good trattoria, offering a small and ever-changing menu of classic Venetian maritime dishes.

ALLA VEDOVA

Calle del Pistor 3912 ☎ 041 528 5324. Mon–Wed & Fri–Sat 11.30am–2.30pm & 6.30–10.30pm, Sun 6.30–10.30pm. MAP PP.88–89, POCKET MAP E10

Located in an alley directly opposite the one leading to the Ca' d'Oro, this long-established little restaurant is fronted by a bar offering a mouthwatering selection of *cicheti* and wines. It's known as one of the best-value places in town (antipasti and main courses from just €10), so reservations are a good idea. No credit cards.

ANICE STELLATO

Fondamenta della Sensa 3272 ☎ 041 720 744. Wed–Sun 12.30–3pm & 6.30pm–midnight. MAP PP.88–89, POCKET MAP E2

Hugely popular with Venetians for the superb, reasonably priced meals and unfussy atmosphere. Situated by one of the northernmost Cannaregio canals, it's rather too remote for most tourists. If you can't get a table – it's frequently booked solid – at least drop by for the excellent *cicheti* at the bar.

DA RIOBA

Fondamenta della Misericordia 2553 ☎ 041 524 4379, ⓦ darioba.com. Tues–Sun 12.30–2.30pm & 7.30–10.30pm. MAP PP.88–89, POCKET MAP F2

This smartly austere *osteria* is another excellent northern

ALLA FONTANA

ANICE STELLATO

Cannaregio restaurant; *Da Rioba* is often full to bursting, especially in summer, when tables are set beside the canal – but the atmosphere is always relaxed. Main courses cost around €20.

PONTINI

Fondamenta Pescheria 1268. Mon–Sat 7am–10.30pm. MAP PP.88–89, POCKET MAP D3

From outside, this looks like any number of ordinary Venetian trattoria-bars, but *Pontini* is far from ordinary: the well-priced menu (around €30 per head) consists of classic Venetian *osteria* food, and the quality is excellent. Not only that, the staff are perhaps the most welcoming in Venice.

VINI DA GIGIO

Fondamenta S. Felice 3628a ☎ 041 528 5140. Wed–Sun noon–2.30pm & 7.30–10.30pm. MAP PP.88–89, POCKET MAP E10

This family-run restaurant may now be firmly on the tourist map but it has managed to retain its authenticity and eating here is still good value (by Venetian standards), even if prices have crept up in recent years.

Bars

AL PARLAMENTO

Fondamenta Savorgnan 511 ☎ 041 244 0214. Mon–Sat 7.30am–1.30am, Sun 9am–1.30am. MAP PP.88–89, POCKET MAP C2

This spacious and friendly bar has recently been refurbished, and is now the area's smartest, with pale wood furnishings and lengths of rope slung across the ceiling to impart a touch of maritime cool. Good snacks and cocktails, and live music too.

LA CANTINA

Strada Nova 3689. Mon–Sat 11am–11pm. MAP PP.88–89, POCKET MAP E10

Welcoming *enoteca* with a good range of wines, substantial and excellent snacks, its own custom-brewed beer, and outdoors seating.

UN MONDO DIVINO

Salizzada San Canciano 5984a. Daily 10am–11.30pm. MAP PP.88–89, POCKET MAP G11

Occupying a marble-fronted old butcher's shop, this brilliant little *bácaro* has rapidly built up a great reputation for its fantastic array of *cicheti*, its choice selection of wines, and the warmth of its staff. Prices are high, however.

Classical music

TEATRO MALIBRAN

Corte Milion 5873 🌐 www.teatrolafenice.it. MAP PP.88–89, POCKET MAP G11–12

Along with the Fenice, this is the city's main venue for big-name classical concerts (and occasional jazz/rock). Tickets cost between €25 and €70 and can be bought on the night at the box office or from the same outlets as the Fenice (see p.57).

Central Castello

Bordering San Marco on one side and spreading across the city from Cannaregio in the west to the housing estates of Sant'Elena in the east, Castello is so unwieldy a *sestiere* that we've cut it in two for the purposes of this guide – this chapter starts off at its western border and stops in the east at a line drawn north from the landmark Pietà church.

In terms of its importance, Castello's central building is the immense Gothic church of Santi Giovanni e Paolo (or Zanipolo), the pantheon of Venice's doges. The museums lie in the southern zone – the Querini-Stampalia picture collection, the museum at San Giorgio dei Greci, and the Museo Diocesano's sacred art collection. This southern area's dominant building is the majestic San Zaccaria, right by the southern waterfront and Venice's main promenade, the Riva degli Schiavoni.

SANTI GIOVANNI E PAOLO

Mon–Sat 9am–6pm, Sun noon–6pm. €2.50. MAP P.102, POCKET MAP H11

Like the Frari, the massive Gothic brick edifice of Santi Giovanni e Paolo – slurred by the Venetian dialect into **San Zanipolo** – was built for one of the mendicant orders, whose

THE RIVA DEGLI SCHIAVONI

social mission (preaching to and tending the sick and the poor) required a lot of space for their congregations. The first church built on this site was begun in 1246 after **Doge Giacomo Tiepolo** (d.1249) was inspired by a dream to donate the land to the Dominicans. Tiepolo's simple sarcophagus is outside, on the left of the door, next to that of his son Doge Lorenzo Tiepolo (d.1275); the cavernous interior – approximately 90m long, 38m wide at the transepts, 33m high in the centre – houses the tombs of some 25 other doges.

Most of the **entrance wall** is given over to the glorification of the Mocenigo family, with three monuments to fifteenth-century doges from this dynasty. But the finest funerary monuments are in the **chancel**, where Doge Michele Morosini, who ruled for just four months before dying of plague in 1382, is buried in the tomb at the front on the right, a work which to Ruskin's eyes showed "the exactly intermediate condition of feeling between the pure calmness of early Christianity, and the boastful pomp of the Renaissance faithlessness". Full-blown Renaissance pomp is represented by the **tomb of Doge Andrea Vendramin** (d.1478), diagonally opposite, while one of the earliest examples of Renaissance style in Venice – Pietro Lombardo's **tomb for Doge Pasquale Malipiero** (d.1462) – is in the left aisle, to the left of the sacristy. (The sacristy itself contains an excellent painting, Alvise Vivarini's *Christ Carrying the Cross*.) The Lombardo family were also responsible for the tombs of Doge Giovanni Mocenigo and Doge Pietro Mocenigo, to the right and left of the main door. Close by, the second altar of the right aisle is adorned by one of Zanipolo's finest paintings, **Giovanni Bellini**'s *SS Vincent Ferrer, Christopher and Sebastian*.

At the top of the right aisle, Giambattista Piazzetta's *St Dominic in Glory* covers the vault of the **Cappella di San Domenico**, alongside which is a tiny shrine containing a relic of St Catherine of Siena. She died in 1380 and her body promptly entered the relic market – most of it is in Rome, but her head is in Siena, one foot is here, and lesser relics are scattered about Italy. Round the corner, in the south transept, two other superb paintings hang close together: a *Coronation of the Virgin* attributed to Cima da Conegliano and Giovanni Martini da Udine, and Lorenzo Lotto's *St Antonine* (1542).

And don't miss the **Cappella del Rosario**, at the end of the north transept. In 1867 a fire destroyed its paintings by Tintoretto, as well as Giovanni Bellini's *Madonna* and Titian's *Martyrdom of St Peter*, San Zanipolo's two most celebrated paintings. A lengthy restoration made use of surviving fragments and installed other pieces such as Veronese's ceiling panels and an *Adoration* on the left of the door.

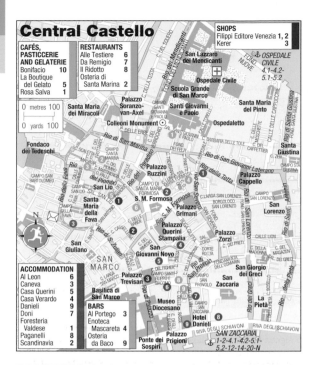

Central Castello

THE COLLEONI MONUMENT

MAP ABOVE, POCKET MAP H11

When he died in 1475, the mercenary captain **Bartolomeo Colleoni** left a legacy of some seven hundred thousand ducats to the Venetian state. But there was a snag: the Signoria could have the money only if an **equestrian monument** to him were erected in the square before San Marco – an unthinkable proposition to Venice's rulers, with their cult of anonymity. The problem was circumvented with a fine piece of disingenuousness, by which Colleoni's will was taken to permit the raising of the statue before the Scuola di San Marco, rather than the Basilica. **Andrea Verrocchio**'s statue wasn't finally unveiled until 1496, but the wait was certainly worth it: this idealized image of steely masculinity is one of the masterpieces of Renaissance sculpture.

THE SCUOLA GRANDE DI SAN MARCO

ⓦ scuolagrandesanmarco.it. Tues–Sat 9.30am–1pm & 2–5pm; pharmacy open Mon 2–5pm. €3. . MAP ABOVE, POCKET MAP H11

Colleoni's backdrop, the Scuola Grande di San Marco, now provides a sumptuous facade and foyer for Venice's hospital. The facade was started by Pietro Lombardo and Giovanni Buora in 1487, half a century after the *scuola* moved here from its original home in the Santa Croce *sestiere*, and was finished in 1495 by Mauro Codussi. Taken as a whole, the panels by Tullio and Antonio Lombardo might not quite create the intended illusion, but they are nonetheless charming.

THE SCUOLA GRANDE DI SAN MARCO

Inside, the entrance hall was designed by Mauro Codussi, who also designed the staircase that leads up to the Sala Capitolare, whose spectacular golden ceiling hangs over a collection of medical instruments and books. The Tintoretto paintings that used to adorn the walls are now in the Accademia and the Brera, but two works by Tintoretto and his son are still in place. The adjacent Sala dell'Albergo, also stripped of its pictures by Gentile and Giovanni Bellini, among others, now has amazingly accurate digital reproductions in their place. Next door, the Scuola di Santa Maria della Pace is now home to a collection of specimens of anatomical pathology and a reconstruction of an old pharmacy.

THE OSPEDALETTO

MAP OPPOSITE, POCKET MAP J4

Another hospital block is attached to Longhena's church of the Ospedaletto, which stands immediately to the east of Zanipolo. Known more properly as **Santa Maria dei Derelitti**, the Ospedaletto was founded in 1528 to provide care for the desperate peasants who were forced by famine to flee the mainland that year. The church itself, with its leering giants' heads and over-ripe decorations, drew Ruskin's wrath, who called it "the most monstrous" building in the city.

The much less extravagant **interior** has a series of eighteenth-century paintings high on the walls above the arches, one of which – *The Sacrifice of Isaac* – is an early Giambattista Tiepolo (fourth on the right). The adjoining **music room**, frescoed in the eighteenth century, is still used for concerts.

At other times, the only way to see inside the Ospedaletto is by booking a private tour – details are on Ⓦwww .scalabovolo.org.

SANTA MARIA FORMOSA

Mon–Sat 10am–5pm. €3 or Chorus Pass.
MAP P.102, POCKET MAP H12–13

The church of **Santa Maria Formosa**, which occupies one of the city's largest and most attractive squares, was founded in the seventh century by San Magno, Bishop of Oderzo, who was guided by a dream in which he saw the Madonna *formosa* – a word which most closely translates as buxom and beautiful. Outside, the most unusual feature is the face at the base of the campanile: it's been argued that it is both a talisman against the evil eye and a piece of clinical realism, portraying a man with a disorder of the sort that disfigured Joseph Merrick, the so-called Elephant Man. The church contains two good paintings. Entering from the west side, the first one you'll see is Bartolomeo Vivarini's triptych of *The Madonna of the Misericordia* (1473), in a nave chapel on the right-hand side of the church. Nearby, closer to the main altar, is Palma il Vecchio's *St Barbara* (1522–24), praised by George Eliot as "an almost unique presentation of a hero-woman".

SANTA MARIA FORMOSA

PALAZZO GRIMANI

ⓦ palazzogrimani.org. Mon 8.15am–2pm, Tues–Sun 8.15am–7.15pm. €6 or €9 with Accademia. MAP P.102, POCKET MAP H13

South of Santa Maria Formosa, if you turn first left off Ruga Giuffa you'll be confronted by the gargantuan sixteenth-century **Palazzo Grimani**, once owned by the branch of the Grimani family whose collection of antiquities became the basis of the Museo Archeologico. The neo-Roman interior, featuring some of the most spectacular rooms in the city, has been beautifully restored and furnished with a miscellany of *objets d'art*. Special exhibitions are often held here too.

SANTA MARIA DELLA FAVA

Mon–Sat 8.30am–noon & 4.30–7.30pm.
MAP P.102, POCKET MAP G13

Between Santa Maria Formosa and the Rialto stands the church of **Santa Maria della Fava** (or Santa Maria della Consolazione), whose peculiar name derives from a sweet cake called a *fava* (bean), once an All Souls' Day speciality of a local baker and still a seasonal treat. On the first altar on the right stands Giambattista Tiepolo's early *Education of the Virgin* (1732); on the other side of the church there's *The Madonna and St Philip Neri*, painted five years earlier by the influential Giambattista Piazzetta.

PALAZZO QUERINI-STAMPALIA

ⓦ querinistampalia.it. Tues–Sun 10am–6pm €10. MAP P.102, POCKET MAP H13

On the south side of Campo di Santa Maria Formosa, a footbridge over a narrow canal leads into the **Palazzo Querini-Stampalia**, home of the Pinacoteca Querini-Stampalia. Although there is a batch of Renaissance pieces – such as Palma il Vecchio's marriage portraits of Francesco Querini and Paola Priuli Querini (for whom the palace was built), and Giovanni **Bellini**'s *Presentation in the Temple* – the general tone of the collection is set by the culture of eighteenth-century Venice, a period to which much of the palace's decor belongs. The winningly inept pieces by **Gabriel Bella** form a comprehensive record of Venetian social life in that century, and the more accomplished genre paintings of **Pietro and Alessandro Longhi** feature prominently as well. One other notable aspect of this museum is that its ground-floor rooms (where good contemporary art shows are often held) were brilliantly refashioned in the 1960s by Carlo Scarpa, who also designed the entrance bridge and the garden – an ensemble that constitutes one of Venice's extremely rare examples of first-class modern architecture.

THE MUSEO DIOCESANO

Tues–Sun 10am–6pm. €4. MAP P.102. POCKET MAP H14

Beside the Rio di Palazzo, at the back of the Palazzo Ducale, stands the early fourteenth-century cloister of **Sant'Apollonia**, the only Romanesque cloister in the city. Fragments from the Basilica di San Marco dating back to the ninth century are displayed here, and a miscellany of sculptural pieces from other churches are on show in the adjoining **Museo Diocesano d'Arte Sacra**. In addition, freshly restored works from other collections or churches sometimes pass through here, giving the museum an edge of unpredictability. A late fifteenth-century Crucifix from San Pietro di Castello is perhaps the most impressive single item, but this is very much one of the city's minor museums.

SAN ZACCARIA

Mon–Sat 10am–noon & 4–6pm, Sun 4–6pm.
MAP P.102, POCKET MAP J6

East of Sant'Apollonia, the Salizzada di San Provolo, leading east out of Campo Santi Filippo e Giacomo, runs straight to the elegant **Campo San Zaccaria**, a spot with a bloody past. In 864 **Doge Pietro Tradonico** was murdered in the campo as he returned from vespers, and in 1172 **Doge Vitale Michiel II**, having not only blundered in peace negotiations with the Byzantine empire but also brought the plague back with him from Constantinople, was murdered as he fled for the sanctuary of San Zaccaria.

Founded in the ninth century as a shrine for the body of Zaccharias, father of John the Baptist, the church of San Zaccaria had already been rebuilt several times when, in 1444, Antonio Gambello embarked on a rebuilding that was concluded some seventy years later by Mauro Codussi, who took over the facade from the first storey upwards. The end result is a distinctively Venetian mixture of Gothic and Renaissance styles.

The interior's notable architectural feature is its **ambulatory**: unique in Venice, it might have been built to accommodate the annual ritual of the doges' Easter Sunday visit. Nearly every inch of wall surface is hung with seventeenth- and eighteenth-century paintings, all of them outshone by Giovanni **Bellini**'s *Madonna and Four Saints* (1505), on the second altar on the left. The €1.50 fee payable to enter the Cappella di Sant'Atanasio and Cappella di San Tarasio (off the right aisle) is well worth it for the three wonderful altarpieces by Antonio Vivarini and Giovanni d'Alemagna (all 1443). Steps descend to the perpetually waterlogged ninth-century crypt, the burial place of eight early doges.

THE RIVA DEGLI SCHIAVONI

MAP P.102, POCKET MAP H15/H6–K6

The broad Riva degli Schiavoni, stretching from the edge of the Palazzo Ducale almost as far as the Arsenale canal, is usually thronged with promenading tourists and passengers hurrying to and from its vaporetto stops, threading through the souvenir stalls and past the wares of the illicit street vendors. The Riva has long been one of Venice's smart addresses. Petrarch and his daughter lived at no. 4145 in 1362–67, and Henry James stayed at no. 4161, battling against constant distractions to finish *The Portrait of a Lady*. George Sand, Charles Dickens, Proust, Wagner and the ever-present Ruskin all checked in at the *Hotel Danieli* (see p.146).

BELLINI'S MADONNA AND FOUR SAINTS, SAN ZACCARIA

LA PIETÀ

Thurs–Sun 10am–6pm. €3. MAP P.102, POCKET MAP J6

The main eyecatcher on the Riva is the white facade of **Santa Maria della Visitazione**, known as La Pietà. **Vivaldi** wrote many of his finest pieces for the orphanage attached to the church, where he worked as violin-master (1704–18) and choirmaster (1735–38). During Vivaldi's second term, Massari won a competition to rebuild the church, and it's probable that the composer advised him on acoustics. Building began in 1745 (after Vivaldi's death), and when the interior was completed in 1760 it was regarded more as a concert hall than a church. The white and gold interior is crowned by a superb ceiling painting, *The Glory of Paradise* by Giambattista Tiepolo, who also painted the ceiling panel above the altar. The Pietà's in-house orchestra plays Vivaldi here two or three times a week, with the *Four Seasons* always on the bill; the management charges visitors €3 for a look inside.

THE GREEK QUARTER

MAP P.102, POCKET MAP J6

To the north of La Pietà, the campanile of **San Giorgio dei Greci** (Mon & Wed–Sat 9.30am–12.30pm & 2.30–4.30pm, Sun 9am–1pm) tilts hazardously canalwards. The **Greek** presence in Venice was strong from the eleventh century, and became stronger still after the Turkish seizure of Constantinople. Built a century later, the church has Orthodox architectural elements including a *matroneo* (women's gallery) and an iconostasis that completely cuts off the high altar. The icons on the screen include a few Byzantine pieces dating back as far as the twelfth century.

The adjacent Scuola di San Nicolò dei Greci now houses the **Museo di Dipinti Sacri Bizantini** (daily 9am–5pm; €4), a collection of predominantly fifteenth- to eighteenth-century icons, many of them by the *Madoneri*, the school of Greek and Cretan artists working in Venice in that period.

Shops

FILIPPI EDITORE VENEZIA

Caselleria 5284 & Calle del Paradiso 5763
Ⓦ libreriaeditricefilippi.com. Mon–Sat
9am–12.30pm & 3–7.30pm. MAP P.102,
POCKET MAP G13

The family-run Filippi business produces a vast range of Venice-related facsimile editions, including Francesco Sansovino's sixteenth-century guide to the city (the first city guide ever published), and sells an amazing stock of books about Venice in its two shops.

KERER

Palazzo Trevisan-Cappello, on Rio Canonica
Ⓦ kerer.it. Mon–Sat 10am–6pm, Sun
10am–12.30pm. MAP P.102, POCKET MAP H14

Occupying part of a huge palazzo at the rear of the Basilica di San Marco, this vast showroom sells a wide range of lace, both affordable and exclusive.

Cafés, pasticcerie and gelaterie

BONIFACIO

Calle degli Albanesi 4237. Mon–Wed & Fri
6.30am–7pm, Sat & Sun 7.30am–7pm. MAP
P.102, POCKET MAP H14

Compact and wonderful café-bar-*pasticceria*, a few minutes' stroll east of the Piazza.

LA BOUTIQUE DEL GELATO

Salizzada S. Lio 5727. Daily: June–Sept
10am–11.30pm; Oct, Nov & mid-Feb to May
10.30am–8.30pm. MAP P.102, POCKET MAP G13

Top-grade ice creams – maybe even the very best in Venice, – are available at this small outlet.

KERER

ROSA SALVA

Campo Santi Giovanni e Paolo 6779
Ⓦ www.rosasalva.it. Mon, Tues & Thurs–Sun
7.30am–8.30pm. MAP P.102, POCKET MAP H12

With its marble-topped bar and outside tables within the shadow of Zanipolo, this is the most characterful of the city's three *Rosa Salva* branches. The coffee and home-made ice cream are superb.

Restaurants

ALLE TESTIERE

Calle Mondo Nuovo 5801 ☎ 041 522 7220,
Ⓦ www.osterialletestiere.it. Tues–Sat
noon–3pm & 7–11pm; closed mid-July to
mid-Aug. MAP P.102, POCKET MAP H13

Very small, very special and rather pricey seafood restaurant in the alley on the other side of the canal from the front of Santa Maria Formosa, with an ever-changing menu and a superb wine selection. In the evening there are sittings at 7pm and 9pm, to handle the demand – booking is essential.

DA REMIGIO

Salizzada dei Greci 3416 ☎ 041 523 0089. Mon 12.30–2.30pm, Wed–Sun 1–2.30pm & 7.30–10pm. MAP P.102, POCKET MAP J5

Well-established trattoria, serving excellent fish dishes and gorgeous home-made gnocchi. The wine list is outstanding too. Be sure to book – the locals (and increasingly tourists) pack this place every night. While many other restaurants ramped up their prices in recently, it remains good value.

IL RIDOTTO

Campo Santi Filippo e Giacomo 4509 ☎ 041 520 0280, ⓦ ilridotto.com. Mon, Tues & Fri–Sun 12.30–2pm & 7–10.30pm, Thurs 7–10.30pm. MAP P.102, POCKET MAP H14

The best restaurant within a short radius of the Piazza. À la carte, you'll get little change from €100 per person, but it has some excellent set menus – just €28 at lunch, and in the evenings there are two five-course €80 tasting menus.

OSTERIA DI SANTA MARINA

Campo Santa Marina 5911 ☎ 041 528 5239, ⓦ osteriadisantamarina.com. Tues–Sat 12.30–2.30pm & 7.30–10pm. MAP P.102, POCKET MAP G12

Highly rated by most Italian food magazines, this is a very slick and impressive modern operation offering imaginative variants on Venetian maritime standards, such as raw fish starters. The wine list is impressive too. Expect to pay €25–30 for your main course.

Bars and snacks

AL PORTEGO

Calle Malvasia 6015. Daily 11am–3pm & 5.30–10pm. MAP P.102, POCKET MAP G12

In the middle of the day this

AL PORTEGO

bar is crammed with customers eating *cicheti*, and in the evening there's often a queue for a place at one of the tiny tables, where some well-prepared basics (pasta, risotto, etc) are served. No reservations are taken.

ENOTECA MASCARETA

Calle Lunga Santa Maria Formosa 5183. Daily 7am–1am. MAP P.102, POCKET MAP H12

Excellent wine bar with delicious *cicheti* and a small menu of more substantial food. The same management runs the nearby *Mascaron* restaurant (at no. 5225), which also has interesting *cicheti* at the bar, but foreigners can sometimes get quite rude treatment there – which is a shame, as the food is good.

OSTERIA DA BACO

Calle delle Rasse 4620. Tues–Sun noon–2pm & 7–10pm. MAP P.102, POCKET MAP H14

Da Baco is a first-choice place for a quick bite after you've toured the Palazzo Ducale – it's the nearest genuine old-style *osteria* to the Piazza, with an excellent range of sandwiches and other snacks.

Eastern Castello

Sights are thinly spread in the eastern section of the Castello *sestiere*, and a huge bite is taken out of the area by the dockyards of the Arsenale, yet the slab of the city immediately to the west of the Arsenale contains places that shouldn't be ignored – the Renaissance San Francesco della Vigna, for example, and the Scuola di San Giorgio degli Schiavoni, with its endearing cycle of paintings by Carpaccio. And although the mainly residential area beyond the Arsenale has little to offer in the way of cultural monuments other than the ex-cathedral of San Pietro di Castello and the church of Sant'Elena, the whole length of the waterfront gives spectacular panoramas of the city.

SAN FRANCESCO DELLA VIGNA

Mon–Sat 8am–12.30pm & 3–6.30pm, Sun 3–6.30pm. MAP OPPOSITE, POCKET MAP K4

The area that lies to the **east of San Zanipolo** is not an attractive district at first sight, but carry on east along Barbaria delle Tole for just a couple of minutes and a striking Renaissance facade blocks your way. The ground occupied by San Francesco

della Vigna has a hallowed place in the mythology of Venice, as according to tradition it was around here that the angel appeared to St Mark to tell him that the lagoon islands were to be his final resting place. Begun in 1534, the present building was much modified in the course of its construction. Palladio was brought in to provide the facade, a feature that looks like

SAN FRANCESCO DELLA VIGNA

| 0 | metres | 100 |
| 0 | yards | 100 |

ACCOMMODATION
| Gabrielli | 2 |
| La Residenza | 1 |

RESTAURANTS
Al Covo	4
Al Garanghelo	5
Corte Sconta	3
CoVino	2

BAR
| Alla Rampa | 1 |

Eastern Castello

something of an afterthought from the side, but which must have been stunning at the time. The **interior** has some fine works of art, notably a glowingly colourful *Madonna and Child Enthroned* by Antonio da Negroponte (right transept), marvellous sculpture by the Lombardo family in the Giustiniani chapel (left of the chancel), and a *Sacra Conversazione* by Veronese (last chapel of the left aisle). A door at the end of the transept leads to a pair of tranquil fifteenth-century cloisters, via the **Cappella Santa**, which has a *Madonna and Child* by Giovanni Bellini and assistants.

THE SCUOLA DI SAN GIORGIO DEGLI SCHIAVONI

Mon 2.45–6pm, Tues–Sat 9.15am–1pm & 2.45–6pm, Sun 9.15am–1pm. €5. MAP ABOVE, POCKET MAP J5

Venice has two brilliant cycles of pictures by **Vittore Carpaccio**, one of the most disarming of Venetian artists – one is in the Accademia, the other in the Scuola di San Giorgio degli Schiavoni, the confraternity of Venice's Slavic community. The cycle illustrates mainly the lives of the Dalmatian patron saints – George, Tryphone and Jerome. As always with Carpaccio, what holds your attention is not so much the main event as the incidental details with which he packs the scene, such as the limb-strewn feeding-ground of St George's dragon, or the endearing little white dog in *The Vision of St Augustine* (he was writing to St Jerome when a vision told him of Jerome's death).

111

SAN GIOVANNI IN BRÁGORA

Mon–Sat 9am–noon & 4–7pm, Sun 4–7pm.
MAP P.111, POCKET MAP K6

San Giovanni in Brágora is probably best known to Venetians as the baptismal church of Antonio Vivaldi. The church is dedicated to the Baptist, and some people think that its strange suffix is a reference to a region from which some relics of the saint were once brought; others link the name to the old dialect words for mud (*brago*) and backwater (*gora*). The present structure was begun in 1475, and its best paintings were created within a quarter-century of the rebuilding: a triptych by **Bartolomeo Vivarini**, on the wall between the first and second chapels on the right; a *Resurrection* by **Alvise Vivarini**, to the left of the sacristy door; and two paintings by **Cima da Conegliano** – a *SS Helen and Constantine*, to the right of the sacristy door, and a *Baptism* on the high altar.

THE ARSENALE

MAP P.111, POCKET MAP K5–L6

A corruption of the Arabic *darsina* (house of industry), the very name of the Arsenale is indicative of the strength of Venice's links with the eastern Mediterranean, and the workers of these dockyards and factories were the foundations upon which the city's maritime supremacy rested. By the 1420s it had become the base for some 300 shipping companies, operating around 3000 vessels of 200 tons or more; at the Arsenale's zenith, around the middle of the sixteenth century, its wet and dry docks, its rope and sail factories, its ordnance depots and gunpowder mills

San Pietro and Sant'Elena

GATEWAY TO THE ARSENALE

224-oar fighting galley and the last *Bucintoro* (the state ceremonial galley) – share space with miscellaneous armaments and other naval items.

VIA GARIBALDI AND SAN PIETRO DI CASTELLO

MAP OPPOSITE, POCKET MAP L7

In 1808 the greater part of the canal connecting the Bacino di San Marco to the broad northeastern inlet of the Canale di San Pietro was filled in to form what is now Via Garibaldi, the widest street in the city and the social hub of the eastern district. Via Garibaldi points the way to the island of **San Pietro**, one of the first parts of central Venice to be inhabited. Nowadays this is a workaday district where the repairing of boats is the main occupation, yet it was once the eccleslastical centre of Venice, having been the seat of the **Patriarch of Venice** until 1807. As with the Arsenale, the history of San Pietro is somewhat more interesting than what you can see. The present San Pietro di Castello (Mon–Sat 10am–5pm; €3 or Chorus Pass) is a fairly charmless church, its most interesting features being the stone-clad and precarious **campanile**, and the so-called **Throne of St Peter** (in the right aisle), a marble seat made in the thirteenth century from an Arabic funeral stone cut with texts from the Koran. A late work by Veronese, *SS John the Evangelist, Peter and Paul,* hangs by the entrance to the Cappello Lando (left aisle), where you'll find a bust of St Lorenzo Giustiniani, the first Patriarch of Venice. Giustiniani, who died in 1456, lies in the glass case within the elaborate high altar, which was designed by Longhena.

employed a total of 16,000 men – equal to the population of a major town of the period.

There is no public access to the Arsenale, but you can inspect the magnificent **gateway** at close quarters. The first structure in Venice to employ the classical vocabulary of Renaissance architecture, it is guarded by four photogenic lions brought here from Greece: the two furthest on the right probably came from the Lion Terrace at Delos, and date from around the sixth century BC; the larger pair were stolen from Piraeus in 1687 by Francesco Morosini.

THE MUSEO STORICO NAVALE

April–Oct Mon–Thurs 8.45am–1.30pm, Fri & Sat 8.45am–5.30pm, Sun 10am–5.30pm; Nov–March closes 5pm Fri–Sun. €5. MAP P.111, POCKET MAP K6–L6

Documenting every facet of Venice's naval history, the Museo Storico Navale is a somewhat diffuse museum, but a selective tour is an essential supplement to a walk round the Arsenale district. Models of Venetian craft and battleships – from the gondola to the

THE PUBLIC GARDENS AND THE BIENNALE SITE

MAP P.112, POCKET MAP M8

Stretching from Via Garibaldi to the Rio di Sant'Elena, the arc of green spaces formed by the **Giardini Garibaldi**, **Giardini Pubblici** and **Parco delle Rimembranze** provide a remedy for the claustrophobia that overtakes many visitors to Venice at some point. Largely obscured by the trees are the rather more extensive grounds belonging to the Biennale, a dormant zone except when the art and architecture shindigs are in progress (in the summer of odd- and even-numbered years respectively; see p.158). Various countries have built permanent pavilions for their Biennale representatives, forming a unique colony that features work by some of the great names of modern architecture and design, such as Alvar Aalto, Gerrit Thomas Rietveld and Carlo Scarpa.

SANT'ELENA

Mon–Sat 5–7pm. MAP P.112

The island of Sant'Elena, the city's eastern limit, was greatly enlarged during the Austrian administration, partly to furnish accommodation and exercise grounds for the occupying troops. Its sole monument is Sant'Elena church, founded in the thirteenth century to house the body of St Helena, Constantine's mother. Approached between the walls of the naval college and the ramshackle home of Venice's football team, it's worth visiting for the fine **doorway**, an ensemble incorporating the **monument to Vittore Cappello**, captain-general of the republic's navy in the 1460s, showing him kneeling before St Helena. Inside the church, a chapel on the right enshrines the alleged remains of Helena, whose body is more generally believed to lie in a tomb in Rome's church of Santa Maria in Aracoeli.

SANT'ELENA

Restaurants

AL COVO

Campiello della Pescaria 3968 ☎ 041 522 3812, ⓦ www.ristorantealcovo.com. Mon–Tues & Fri–Sun 12.45–2pm & 7.30–10pm; closed mid-Dec to mid-Jan. MAP P.111, POCKET MAP K6

Located in a backwater to the east of Campo Bandiera e Moro, *Covo* is one of Venice's foodie havens, with a consistently high reputation that's maintained partly through its refusal to use frozen or farmed fish. Main courses are €25–35, and there's a delicious *menu degustazione* for €75.

AL GARANGHELO

Via Garibaldi 1621 ☎ 041 520 4967, ⓦ garanghelo.com. Mon & Wed–Sun 8am–midnight. MAP P.111, POCKET MAP L7

Run by brothers Lucio and Simone, this *osteria* is the best place to eat on Via Garibaldi. Lucio – who also runs the nearby *Giorgione* – often regales his guests with Venetian songs, so it's not the best place for a quiet evening, but the food is good and not expensive, with mains in the region of €15.

CORTE SCONTA

Calle del Pestrin 3886 ☎ 041 522 7024. Tues–Sat 12.30–2pm & 7pm–midnight. MAP P.111, POCKET MAP K6

Secreted in a lane to the east of San Giovanni in Brágora, this restaurant is one of Venice's finest. The exceptionally pleasant staff tend to make it difficult to resist ordering the day's specials, which could easily result in a bill in the region of €80–90 each – and it would be just about the best meal you could get in Venice for that price. Booking several days in advance is essential for most of the year.

CORTE SCONTA

COVINO

Calle del Pestrin 3829 ☎ 041 241 2705, ⓦ covinovenezia.com. Mon & Thurs–Sun 12.30–3pm & 7–10.30pm, Wed 7–10.30pm. MAP P.111, POCKET MAP K6

This fourteen-seat micro-restaurant is regarded by some as one of the Venice's best new restaurants, though others find it a little pretentious. But nobody would dispute that it's unlike anywhere else in the city, and is serious about its food. You pay a fixed €36 for three courses and a glass of wine; the menu changes daily. Add on extra drinks and you'll be paying over €50 a head. No credit cards. Booking essential.

Bar

ALLA RAMPA

Salizzada S. Antonin 3607. Mon–Sat 8am–10pm. MAP P.111, POCKET MAP K6

Shabby and totally authentic bar, which has been here for more than forty years. Great for a cheap *ombra* and snack, if you don't mind being the only customer who isn't Venetian.

The Canal Grande

The Canal Grande is Venice's high street, and divides the city in half, with three *sestieri* to the west and three to the east. With the completion of the Calatrava bridge, four bridges now cross the waterway – the Calatrava, plus those at the Scalzi (train station), Rialto and Accademia – but a number of gondola *traghetti* provide additional crossing points at regular intervals, as does the #1 vaporetto, which slaloms from one bank to the other along its entire length. The Canal Grande is almost four kilometres long and varies in width between thirty and seventy metres; it is, however, surprisingly shallow, at no point much exceeding five metres.

The section that follows is principally a selection of Canal Grande palaces. It's arranged as three sections, first covering the bridges, followed by the right bank (to your right as you travel down from the train station) then the left bank; surveying both banks simultaneously is possible only from a seat right at the front or the back of a vaporetto.

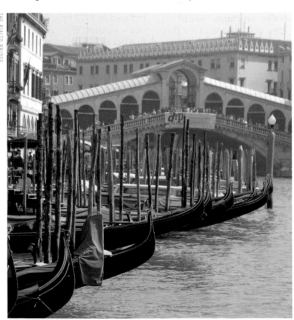

The bridges

THE CALATRAVA AND SCALZI BRIDGES

MAP PP.118–119, POCKET MAP B4 & C4

The newest feature of Venice's cityscape is officially known as the **Ponte della Costituzione**, but Venetians call it the **Ponte di Calatrava**, after its designer, Santiago Calatrava. The single span – an elegant arc of steel, stone and glass – is modelled on the shape of a gondola's hull.

Downstream, more or less in front of the station, lies the **Ponte degli Scalzi**, successor of an iron structure put up by the Austrians in 1858–60; like the one at the Accademia, it was replaced in the early 1930s to give the new steamboats sufficient clearance.

RIALTO BRIDGE

MAP PP.118–119, POCKET MAP F12

The famous Ponte di Rialto superseded a succession of wooden structures – one of Carpaccio's *Miracles of the True Cross*, in the Accademia, shows one of them. The decision to construct a stone bridge was

VIEW THROUGH THE RIALTO BRIDGE

taken in 1524, and eventually the job was awarded to **Antonio da Ponte**. Until 1854, when the Accademia bridge was built, this was the only point at which the Canal Grande could be crossed on foot.

ACCADEMIA BRIDGE

MAP PP.118–119, POCKET MAP C16

As the larger vaporetti couldn't get under the iron Ponte dell' Accademia built by the Austrians in 1854, it was replaced in 1932 by a wooden one – a temporary measure that became permanent with the addition of a reinforcing steel substructure.

Venetian palazzi

Virtually all the surviving Canal Grande palaces were built over a span of about five hundred years, and in the course of that period the **basic plan** varied very little. The typical palace has an entrance hall (the **andron**) on the ground floor, and this runs right through the building, flanked by storage rooms. Above this, there is often a mezzanine – the small rooms on this level were used as offices or, from the sixteenth century onwards, as libraries or living rooms. On the next floor – often the most extravagantly decorated – you find the **piano nobile**, the main living area, arranged as suites on each side of a central hall (**portego**), which runs, like the *andron*, from front to back. The plan of these houses can be read from the outside, where you'll usually see a cluster of large windows in the centre of the facade, between symmetrically placed side windows. Frequently there is a second *piano nobile* above the first – this generally would have been accommodation for relatives or children, though sometimes it was the main living quarters; the attic would contain servants' rooms or storage.

Canal Grande

Palazzo Vendramin-Calergi
Palazzo Soranzo
Palazzo Doria Giovanelli
Rio di Noale
Palazzo Albrizzi

SAN STAE 1-N
San Stae
CORTE BARBARO
Palazzo Gussoni
San Felice
CAMPO SAN FELICE

CANNAREGIO

Ca'Pêsaro
Palazzo Corner della Regina
Ca' d'Oro
CA' D'ORO 1-N
Palazzo Sagredo
Santa Sofia
CAMPO SANTA SOFIA
Santi Apostoli

Palazzo Agnusdio
Palazzo Mocenigo

San Cassiano
Pescheria
Palazzo Mangilli

Santa Maria Mater Domini
CAMPO SAN CASSIANO
Fabbriche Nuove
Ca' da Mosto
Rio San
Palazzo Falier

RIALTO MERCATO 1
San Giovanni Crisostomo

San Giovanni Elemosinario
Rialto Market
Fabbriche Vecchie
Palazzo dei Camerlenghi

SAN POLO
Sant' Aponal
Palazzo Soranzo
San Giacomo di Rialto
Ponte di Rialto
Fondaco dei Tedeschi

Palazzo Corner
CAMPO SAN POLO
San Polo
San Silvestro
RIALTO 1-2-N
San Bartolomeo

Palazzo Donà della Madonnetta
Palazzo Papadopoli
SAN SILVESTRO 1
Canal Grande
Palazzo Dolfin-Manin
Scuola di San Teodoro

Palazzo Bernardo
Palazzo Donà
Palazzo Loredan
San Salvador

Palazzo Cappello-Layard
San Beneto
Palazzo Farsetti
Palazzo Grimani

Palazzo Pisani-Moretta
SANT'ANGELO 1
Palazzo Corner Spinelli
Palazzo Benzon
Museo Fortuny
Teatro Rossini
San Luca
Cassa del Risparmio
CAMPO MANIN

Scala Contarini del Bovolo
Bacino Orseolo

SAN MARCO

Oratorio dell'Annunziata
Ateneo Veneto
San Fantin

Santo Stefano
La Fenice
San Moisè

San Maurizio

Palazzo Loredan
Palazzo Morosini
Palazzo Zaguri
Santa Maria del Giglio
Palazzo Contarini Fasan
Palazzo Giustinian

San Vidal
Palazzo Pisani
Palazzo Pisani

Palazzo Franchetti
Palazzo Corner della Ca'Grande

Ponte dell' Accademia
Palazzo Barbaro
GIGLIO 1

Palazzo Contarini dal Zaffo
Palazzo Dario
SALUTE 1
Punta della Dogana

Cini Collection
Peggy Guggenheim Collection
San Gregorio
Santa Maria della Salute
Seminario Patriarcale
CAMPO DELLA SALUTE

The Right Bank

FONDACO DEI TURCHI

MAP PP.118–119, POCKET MAP C10

Having first passed the green-domed church of **San Simeone Piccolo** and a procession of nondescript buildings, you come to the Fondaco dei Turchi. A private house from the early thirteenth century until 1621, it was then turned over to Turkish traders, who stayed here until 1838. Though it's been over-restored, the building's towers and water-level arcade give a reasonably precise picture of what a Veneto-Byzantine palace would have looked like. See p.79.

CA' PÉSARO

MAP PP.118–119, POCKET MAP D10

A short distance beyond the church of **San Stae** stands the thickly ornamented Ca' Pésaro, bristling with diamond-shaped spikes and grotesque heads. Three houses had to be demolished to make room for this palace and its construction lasted half a century – work finished in 1703, long after the death of the architect, Baldassare Longhena. See p.78.

PALAZZO CORNER DELLA REGINA

MAP PP.118–119, POCKET MAP D10–11

The next large building is the Palazzo Corner della Regina, built in 1724 on the site of the home of **Caterina Cornaro**, Queen of Cyprus, from whom the palace takes its name. It was formerly the *Monte di Pietà*, or municipal pawnshop.

RIALTO MARKET

MAP PP.118–119, POCKET MAP E11–F12

The Rialto markets begin with the neo-Gothic fish market, the **Pescheria**, built in 1907; there's been a fish market here since the fourteenth century. The older buildings that follow it, the **Fabbriche Nuove di Rialto** and (set back from the water) the **Fabbriche Vecchie di Rialto**, are by Sansovino (1555) and Scarpagnino (1522) respectively.

PALAZZO DEI CAMERLENGHI

MAP PP.118–119, POCKET MAP F12

The large building at the base of the Rialto bridge is the Palazzo dei Camerlenghi (c.1525), the former chambers of the Venetian exchequer.

PALAZZO BALBI

MAP PP.118–119, POCKET MAP B14

The Palazzo Balbi, on the Volta del Canal, is a proto-Baroque

VIEW OF THE CANAL GRANDE FROM THE RIALTO BRIDGE

design executed in the 1580s to plans by Alessandro Vittoria, whose sculptures feature in many Venetian churches. Nicolò Balbi is reputed to have moored a boat alongside the building site so that he could watch the work progressing on his house – and died of the chill he consequently caught.

CA' FÓSCARI

MAP PP.118–119, POCKET MAP B14

On the opposite bank stands the Ca' Fóscari (c.1435). The largest private house in Venice at the time of its construction, it was the home of Doge Francesco Fóscari, whose extraordinarily long term of office (34 years) came to an end with his forced resignation. Venice's university now owns the building.

THE PALAZZI GIUSTINIAN

MAP PP.118–119, POCKET MAP B14

The Palazzi Giustinian are a pair of palaces built in the mid-fifteenth century for two brothers who wanted attached but self-contained houses. One of the palazzi was **Wagner**'s home for a while.

CA' REZZONICO

MAP PP.118–119, POCKET MAP B15

Longhena's gargantuan Ca' Rezzonico was begun in 1667 as a commission from the Bon family, but they were obliged to sell the still unfinished palace to the Rezzonico, a family of stupendously wealthy Genoese bankers. Among its subsequent owners was Pen Browning, whose father Robert died here in 1889. See pp.68–69.

PALAZZO VENIER DEI LEONI

MAP PP.118–119, POCKET MAP D16

The Venier family, one of Venice's great dynasties, had

CA' REZZONICO

their main base just beyond the Campo San Vio. In 1759 the Veniers began rebuilding their home, but the Palazzo Venier dei Leoni, which would have been the largest palace on the canal, never progressed further than the first storey – hence its alternative name, **Palazzo Nonfinito**. The stump of the building is occupied by the Guggenheim museum (see pp.60–61).

PALAZZO DARIO

MAP PP.118–119, POCKET MAP D16

The one domestic building of interest between the Guggenheim and the end of the canal is the miniature Palazzo Dario. It was built in the late 1480s, and the multicoloured marbles of the facade are characteristic of the work of the Lombardo family.

DOGANA DI MARE

MAP PP.118–119, POCKET MAP F16

The focal point of this last stretch of the canal is Longhena's masterpiece, **Santa Maria della Salute**, after which comes the Dogana di Mare (Customs House), the Canal Grande's full stop, which now houses the art collection of François Pinault. See also p.61.

The Left Bank

PALAZZO LABIA

MAP PP.118–119, POCKET MAP D3

The boat passes two churches, the **Scalzi** and **San Geremia**, before the first of the major palaces comes into view on the left – the Palazzo Labia. This huge house was completed c.1750, for a madly wealthy Catalan family by the name of Lasbias. The main facade stretches along the Cannaregio canal, but from the Canal Grande you can see how the side wing wraps itself round the campanile of the neighbouring church of San Geremia – such interlocking is common in Venice, to make maximum use of available space. See also p.90.

PALAZZO VENDRAMIN-CALERGI

MAP PP.118–119, POCKET MAP C10/E3

Not far beyond the unfinished church of **San Marcuola** stands the Palazzo Vendramin-Calergi. Begun by Mauro Codussi at the end of the fifteenth century, this was the first Venetian palace built on classical Renaissance lines. The palazzo's most famous resident was Richard Wagner, who died here in February 1883. It's now the home of Venice's casino.

CA' D'ORO

MAP PP.118–119, POCKET MAP E10–11

Incorporating fragments of a thirteenth-century palace that once stood on the site, the gorgeous Ca' d'Oro was built in the 1420s and 30s, and acquired its nickname – "The Golden House" – from the gilding that used to accentuate its carving. (*Ca'* is an abbreviation of *casa di stazio*, meaning the main family home.) See p.94.

CA' DA MOSTO

MAP PP.118–119, POCKET MAP F11

The arches of the first floor of the Ca' da Mosto and the carved panels above them are remnants of a thirteenth-century Veneto-Byzantine building, and are thus among the oldest structures on the Canal Grande.

FONDACO DEI TEDESCHI

MAP PP.118–119, POCKET MAP F12

Just before the Rialto Bridge stands the huge Fondaco dei Tedeschi. Now the main post office, it was once headquarters of the city's German merchants. In 1505 the Fondaco burned down; Giorgione and Titian were commissioned to paint the exterior. The remains of their contribution are now displayed in the Ca' d'Oro.

PALAZZO LOREDAN AND THE PALAZZO FARSETTI

MAP PP.118–119, POCKET MAP E13

The Palazzo Loredan and the adjoining Palazzo Farsetti are heavily restored Veneto-Byzantine palaces of the thirteenth century. They now both house the town hall.

PALAZZO GRIMANI

MAP PP.118–119, POCKET MAP E13

Work began on the immense Palazzo Grimani in 1559, to designs by Sanmicheli, but was not completed until 1575, sixteen years after his death. Ruskin, normally no fan of Renaissance architecture, made an exception for this colossal palace, calling it "simple, delicate, and sublime".

THE MOCENIGO PALAZZI

MAP PP.118–119, POCKET MAP C14

Four houses that once all belonged to the Mocenigo family stand side by side on the **Volta del Canal**, as the Canal Grande's sharpest turn is known: the late sixteenth century **Palazzo Mocenigo-Nero**; the double **Palazzo Mocenigo**, built in the eighteenth century as an extension; and the **Palazzo Mocenigo Vecchio**, a Gothic palace remodelled in the seventeenth century. Byron and his menagerie – a dog, a fox, a wolf and a monkey – lived in the Mocenigo-Nero for a couple of years.

PALAZZO GRASSI

MAP PP.118–119, POCKET MAP C15

The vast palace round the Volta is the Palazzo Grassi, built in 1748–72 by Massari, who supervised the completion of the Ca' Rezzonico. The last great house to be built on the Canal Grande, it's now owned by the art collector and businessman François Pinault, and is used for exhibitions. See p.54.

PALAZZO FRANCHETTI AND PALAZZI BARBARO

MAP PP.118–119, POCKET MAP C16–D16

The huge palazzo at the foot of the bridge is the Palazzo Franchetti, which was built in the fifteenth century and enlarged at the end of the nineteenth. Its neighbours, on the opposite side of the Rio dell'Orso, are the twinned Palazzi Barbaro; the house on the left is early fifteenth century, the other late seventeenth-century. Henry James, Monet, Whistler, Browning and John Singer Sargent were among the luminaries who stayed in the older Barbaro house in the late nineteenth century.

PALAZZO CORNER DELLA CA' GRANDE

MAP PP.118–119, POCKET MAP D16

The palace that used to stand on the site of the Palazzo Corner della Ca' Grande was destroyed when a fire lit to dry out a stock of sugar in the attic ran out of control. Sansovino's replacement, built from 1545 onwards, is notable for the rugged stonework of the lower storey – a prototype for Ca' Pésaro and Ca' Rezzonico.

PALAZZO CONTARINI-FASAN

MAP PP.118–119, POCKET MAP E16

The narrow Palazzo Contarini-Fasan – a mid-fifteenth-century palace with unique wheel tracery on the balconies – is popularly known as "the house of Desdemona", but although the model for Shakespeare's heroine did live in Venice, her association with this house is purely sentimental.

The northern islands

A trip out to the main islands lying to the north of Venice – San Michele, Murano, Burano and Torcello – will reveal the origins of the glass and lace work touted in so many of the city's shops, and give you a glimpse of the origins of Venice itself, embodied in Torcello's magnificent cathedral of Santa Maria dell'Assunta, which is one of the most charismatic buildings in the whole lagoon. These islands – especially Murano – attract a lot of visitors, but the voyage along the islet-dotted water-lanes of the northern lagoon can nonetheless be a great restorative if the crowds in the city are becoming oppressive, and the swathes of low-lying *barèna* (marshland) give a taste of what conditions must have been like for Venice's first settlers.

SAN MICHELE

Church and cemetery daily: April–Sept 7.30am–6pm; Oct–March closes 4pm.
MAP P.126, POCKET MAP J1–K2

The high brick wall around the island of San Michele gives way by the landing stage to the elegant white facade of **San Michele in Isola**, designed by Mauro Codussi in 1469. With this building Codussi quietly revolutionized the architecture of Venice, advancing the principles of Renaissance design in the city and introducing the use of Istrian stone as a material for facades. Easy to carve yet resistant to water, Istrian stone had long been used for damp courses, but never before had anyone clad the entire front of a building in it; after the construction of San Michele,

Boats to the islands

To get to the northern islands, the main vaporetto stop is **Fondamente Nove** (or Nuove), as most of the island services start here or call here. (You can hop on elsewhere in the city, of course – but make sure that the boat is going towards the islands, not away from them.) For **San Michele** and **Murano** only, the circular #4.1 and #4.2 vaporetti both run every twenty minutes from Fondamente Nove, circling Murano before heading back towards Venice; the #4.1 follows an anticlockwise route around the city, the #4.2 a clockwise route. Murano can also be reached by the #3 ("Diretto Murano"), which from around 8am to 6pm runs to the island from Tronchetto via Piazzale Roma and Ferrovia. For **Murano**, **Burano** and **Torcello** the #12 leaves every half-hour from Fondamente Nove for most of the day (hourly early in the morning and evenings), calling first at Murano-Faro before heading on to Mazzorbo and Burano, from where it proceeds, via Treporti, to Punta Sabbioni and the Lido. A shuttle boat runs every fifteen minutes between Burano and Torcello.

most major buildings in Venice were given an Istrian veneer.

The main part of the island, through the cloisters, is covered by the **cemetery** of Venice, established here by a Napoleonic decree which forbade further burials in the centre of the city. Space is at a premium, and most of the Catholic dead of Venice lie here in cramped conditions for just ten years or so, when their bones are dug up and removed

to an ossuary, and the vacated plot is recycled. The city's Protestants, being less numerous, are permitted to stay in their sector indefinitely. In this Protestant section (no. XV) **Ezra Pound**'s grave is marked by a simple slab with his name on it. Adjoining is the Greek and Russian Orthodox area (no. XIV), including the gravestones of **Igor and Vera Stravinsky** and the more elaborate tomb for **Serge Diaghilev**.

Even with its grave-rotation system in operation, the island is reaching full capacity, so it is now being extended, to a design by David Chipperfield, which will place a sequence of formal courtyards lined with wall tombs on the presently unkempt parts of the island, alongside a new funerary chapel and crematorium. It promises to be a beautiful place – and there's a certain appropriateness to the fact that the twenty-first-century's first large-scale addition to the Venetian cityscape will be a cross between a necropolis and a philosopher's retreat.

Murano

—— Vaporetto route

| 0 | metres | 250 |
| 0 | yards | 250 |

Campo Sportivo

Cemetery

Cemetery

Santa Maria degli Angeli

Canal degli Angeli

FOND. SEBASTIANO VENIER

CAMPO S. BERNARDO

C. CORTE COMARE

Canale di San Donato

C. CONTENTE

Santi Maria e Donato

VENIER
4.1-4.2-3-N

Museo del Vetro ❶

RIVA LONGA

MUSEO
4.1-4.2-3-N

Palazzo Trevisan

C. VIVARIAN

Palazzo da Mula

MULA
4.1-4.2

SERENELLA
4.1-4.2-3-N

STRADA VICINALE ORTI

San Pietro Martire

F. ANTONIO COLLEONI

CAMPO SAN STEFANO

FOND. ANDREA NAVAGERO

Palazzo
❷
❸

NAVAGERO
4.1-4.2-3-N

N

FOND. SERENELLA

FONDAMENTA DEI VETRAI

FOND. MANIN

❺

VIALE BRESSAGIO

❸

FOND. SAN GIOVANNI BATTISTA DEI BATTUTI

Canale Grande di Murano

❻

FARO
4.1-4.2-12-13-3

COLONNA
4.1-4.2

CIMITERO
4.1-4.2

San Michele

Fondamente Nove

Burano

Sant'Erasmo

Rio San Matteo

RESTAURANTS

Acquastanca	3
Busa alla Torre	2
La Perla ai Bisatei	1

SHOPS

Barovier & Toso	6	Elle&Elle	4
Berengo	2	Seguso	3
Davide Penso	1	Venini	5

Venetian glass

Because of the risk of fire, Venice's glass furnaces were moved to **Murano** from central Venice in 1291, and thenceforth all possible steps were taken to keep the secrets of the trade locked up on the island. Although Muranese workers had by the seventeenth century gained some freedom of movement, for centuries prior to that any glass-maker who left Murano was proclaimed a traitor, and a few were even hunted down. A fifteenth-century visitor judged that "in the whole world there are no such craftsmen of glass as here", and the Muranese were masters of every aspect of their craft. They were producing spectacles by the start of the fourteenth century, monopolized the European manufacture of mirrors for a long time, and in the early seventeenth century became so proficient at making coloured crystal that a decree was issued forbidding the manufacture of false gems out of glass, as many were being passed off as authentic stones. The traditional style of Murano glass, typified by the multicoloured floral chandeliers sold in showrooms on Murano and round the Piazza, is still very much in demand. However, in recent years there's been turmoil in the glass industry, due to an inundation of cheap Murano-style tableware and ornaments from Asia and eastern Europe. Few of Murano's 250 glass companies remain in Venetian hands – the long-established firm of **Salviati** is French-owned, and even **Venini** has been bought out, by the Royal Copenhagen company.

MURANO

MAP OPPOSITE

Murano nowadays owes its fame entirely to its **glass-blowing industry**, and its main *fondamente* are crowded with shops selling the fruit of the furnaces, some of it fine, much of it repulsive.

From the Colonna vaporetto stop (the first after San Michele) you step onto the Fondamenta dei Vetrai, traditionally the core of the glass industry (as the name suggests) and now the principal tourist trap. Towards the far end is the Dominican church of **San Pietro Martire** (Mon–Fri 8am–7pm, Sat 11am–7pm, Sun noon–5pm), one of only two churches still in service on the island. Begun in 1363 but largely rebuilt after a fire in 1474, it contains a superb altarpiece by **Giovanni Bellini** and a couple of Paolo Veronese pictures.

Murano's one museum is, as you'd expect, devoted to glass. Occupying the seventeenth-century Palazzo Giustinian (formerly home of the Bishop of Torcello), the **Museo del Vetro** (daily: April–Oct 10am–6pm; Nov–March 10am–5pm; €10 or Museum Pass) features pieces dating back to the first century and examples of Murano glass from the fifteenth century onwards. Perhaps the finest single item is the dark blue Barovier marriage cup, dating from around 1470; it's on show in room 2 on the first floor, along with some splendid Renaissance enamelled and painted glass. A separate display, with some captions in English, covers the history of Murano glass techniques – look out for the extraordinary *Murrine*, the method of fusing and stretching differently coloured rods of glass.

The other Murano church, and the main reason for visiting the island today, is **Santi Maria e Donato** (Mon–Sat 9am–noon & 3.30–7pm, Sun 3.30–7pm). It was founded in the seventh century but rebuilt in the twelfth, and is one of the lagoon's best examples of Veneto-Byzantine architecture – the ornate rear apse being particularly fine. The glories of the **interior** are its mosaic floor (dated 1141 in the nave) and the twelfth-century mosaic of the Madonna in the apse.

GLASS MAKER AT WORK ON MURANO

BURANO

MAP OPPOSITE

After the peeling plaster and eroded stonework of the other lagoon settlements, the small, brightly painted houses of Burano come as something of a surprise. Local tradition says that the colours once enabled each fisherman to identify his house from out at sea, but now the colours are used simply for pleasant effect. While many of the men of Burano still depend on the lagoon for their livelihoods, a lot of the island's women sell **lace**, though most of the lace in the shops is imported and machine-made. Real Burano lacemaking is still taught at the **Scuola del Merletto** (Tues–Sun April–Oct 10am–6pm; Nov–March 10am–5pm; €5 or Museum Pass) on Piazza Baldassare Galuppi, which was opened in 1872, when the craft had declined so far that it was left to one woman, Francesca Memo, to transmit the skills to a younger generation. Although the *scuola* is now almost moribund, a few courses are still held here, and pieces produced by its pupils and staff are displayed in the attached **museum**, along with specimens dating back to the sixteenth century.

Opposite the lace school stands the church of **San Martino** (daily 8am–noon & 3–7pm), with its drunken campanile; inside, on the second altar on the left, you'll find a fine *Crucifixion* by Giambattista Tiepolo.

TORCELLO

MAP OPPOSITE

Settled by the very first refugees from the mainland in the fifth century, Torcello became the seat of the Bishop of Altinum in 638 and in the following year its cathedral – the oldest building in the lagoon – was founded. By the fourteenth century its population had peaked at around twenty thousand, but Torcello's canals were now silting up and malaria was rife, and by the end of the fifteenth century Torcello was almost deserted. Today only about thirty people remain in residence.

A Veneto-Byzantine building dating substantially from 1008, the **Cattedrale di Santa Maria dell'Assunta** (daily: March–Oct 10.30am–6pm; Nov–Feb 10am–5pm; €5, or €7 with Museo di Torcello) has evolved

BURANO

Burano and Torcello

| | metres | 250 |
| | yards | 250 |

RESTAURANTS

Al Gatto Nero	3
Da Romano	2
Venissa	1

SHOP

Lidia	1

Palude dei Laghi

Canale di Torcello

Museo · Santa Maria
Santa · dell'Assunta
Fosca

Torcello

TORCELLO
9-N

Canale Borgognoni

Canale Sant' Antonio

Canale di Burano

MAZZORBO
12 N

BURANO 9-12-N

Canale di Mazzorbo

Mazzorbu

Cemetery

Burano

Scuola
del Merletto

San Martino

Santa Caterina

N

from a church founded in the seventh century, of which the crypt and the foundations in front of the façade have survived. The dominant tones of the **interior** come from pink brick, gold-based mosaics and the watery green-grey marble of its columns and panelling, which together cast a cool light on the richly patterned eleventh-century mosaic floor. In the apse a stunning twelfth-century mosaic of the Madonna and Child looks down from above a frieze of the Apostles, which dates from the middle of the previous century. Below the window, at the Madonna's feet, is a much restored image of St Heliodorus, the first Bishop of Altinum, whose sarcophagus lies below the high altar. Mosaic work from the ninth and eleventh centuries adorns the chapel to

the right of the high altar, while the other end of the cathedral is dominated by the tumultuous mosaic of the Apotheosis of Christ and the Last Judgement – created in the twelfth century, but renovated in the nineteenth. Ruskin described the view from the campanile as "one of the most notable scenes in this wide world", a verdict you can test for yourself (unless the tower is undergoing one of its frequent bouts of restoration).

Torcello's other church, **Santa Fosca** (daily 10am–4.30pm; free), was built in the eleventh and twelfth centuries for the body of the martyred St Fosca.

The nearby **Museo di Torcello** (same hours as cathedral; €3, or €7 with cathedral) includes thirteenth-century gold figures, jewellery, mosaic fragments and a mishmash of pieces relating to the history of the area.

Shops: Murano glass

BAROVIER & TOSO

Fondamenta dei Vetrai 27–29 W www
.barovier.com. Mon–Sat 10am–12.30pm &
1–6pm. MAP P.126

This family-run firm can trace its roots back to the fourteenth century. Predominantly traditional designs.

BERENGO

Fondamenta dei Vetrai 109a W berengo.com.
Daily 10am–6pm. MAP P.126

Berengo has pioneered a new approach to Venetian glass manufacture, with foreign artists' designs being vitrified by Murano glass-blowers.

DAVIDE PENSO

Riva Longa 48 W davidepenso.com. Daily
10am–6pm. MAP P.126

The jewellery here is both manufactured and designed by the firm, which specializes in giving a new slant to traditional Murano styles. You can watch glass pieces being made.

ELLE&ELLE

Fondamenta Manin 52 T 041 527 4866.
Daily 10.30am–1pm & 2–6pm. MAP P.126

Stockist of the sleek small-scale glasswork of Nason & Moretti, a long-established Murano firm that consistently produces attractive modern items.

SEGUSO

Viro Fondamenta Manin 77 W segusoviro.com.
Mon–Sat 10.30am–5.30pm. MAP P.126

Archimede Seguso, one of the great figures in the story of Murano glass, founded the firm of Seguso Vetri d'Arte in the 1930s, and the company still has a big shop on the Piazza. Seguso Viro, established by one of Archimede's sons, produces

slightly more eccentric items than the original Seguso firm.

VENINI

Fondamenta Vetrai 47–48 W www.venini
.com. Mon–Sat 9.30am–5.30pm. MAP P.126

One of the more adventurous producers, Venini often employs designers from other fields of the applied arts.

Shops: Burano lace

LIDIA

Via Galuppi 215, Burano T 041 730 052,
W dallalidia.com. Daily 9.30am–6.30pm.
MAP P.129.

The oldest lace shop on the island, Lidia sells new and vintage lacework – a collectible handmade hankie sells for upward of €300, while a hand-embroidered bedsheet goes for more than €4000. The upstairs room is in effect a private museum of Burano lace.

Restaurants

ACQUASTANCA

Fondamenta Manin 48, Murano T 041 319
5125, W acquastanca.it. Mon & Fri 9am–10pm,
Tues–Thurs & Sat 9am–8pm. MAP P. 126.

BURANO LACE

DA ROMANO

This is the best new restaurant to have opened on Murano in many years. It's a good-looking place (lots of bare wood, brick and marble) and the menu is small but classy, with the emphasis on fresh fish. Main courses are in the region of €20, and the front-of-house bar serves fine *cicheti*.

AL GATTO NERO

Fondamenta Giudecca 88, Burano ☎ 041 730 120, ✇ gattonero.com. Tues–Sun noon–2.30pm & 7–10pm. MAP P.129

This outstanding local trattoria has been run since the 1960s by Ruggero Bovo and his wife Lucia, helped by their son Massimiliano. What this family doesn't know about the lagoon's edible delicacies, and wines of the region, isn't worth knowing. Around €40–50 per head.

BUSA ALLA TORRE

Campo S. Stefano 3, Murano ☎ 041 739 662. Tues–Sun 9am–5pm. MAP P.126

By general agreement, this trattoria is the finest restaurant on Murano – unfortunately, though, the kitchen is open for lunch only (noon–3pm). The set menu, at

under €20, is a real bargain. For the rest of the day it functions as a café-bar.

DA ROMANO

Via Galuppi 221, Burano ☎ 041 730 030, ✇ daromano.it. Mon–Fri noon–3pm & 7–10.30pm. MAP P.129

Huge and historic Burano restaurant, whose refined fish and seafood dishes have no lack of local devotees – the fish-broth risotto is famous. The columned dining room is impressive too. Expect to pay around €50 per person.

LA PERLA AI BISATEI

Campo San Bernardo 1e, Murano ☎ 041 739 528. Daily noon–3pm. MAP P.126

This is a basic but very good neighbourhood bar-trattoria, tucked into a corner of the island that very few tourists pass through. Pasta dishes, risotto and *frittura* form the core of the menu, and prices are amazingly low – many mains are under €10. No credit cards.

VENISSA

Fondamenta Santa Caterina 3, Mazzorbo ☎ 041 52 72 281, ✇ venissa.it. Restaurant April–Oct Mon & Wed–Sun noon–3pm & 7–11pm. Wine bar May–Oct Mon, Tues & Thurs–Sun 11am–11pm; Nov–April same days noon–3pm & 7–11pm. MAP P.129

Chef Antonia Klugmann uses the resources of the lagoon and the restaurant's garden and vineyard to create a menu that mixes the traditional and the innovative to brilliant effect. The dining room is stylishly modern and intimate (booking is essential), and there are tables outside in good weather. Main courses hover around the €40 mark, and there's a fabulous nine-course tasting menu for about €100. The food is simpler and less expensive in the adjoining wine bar – reckon on €40 per person.

The southern islands

The section of the lagoon to the south of the city, enclosed by the long islands of the Lido and Pellestrina, has fewer outcrops of solid land than its northern counterpart. The nearer islands are the more interesting: the Palladian churches of San Giorgio and La Giudecca (linked by the #2 vaporetto) are among Venice's most significant Renaissance monuments, while the alleyways of La Giudecca are full of reminders of the city's manufacturing past. The Venetian tourist industry began with the development of the Lido, which has now been eclipsed by the city itself as a holiday destination, yet still draws thousands of people to its beaches each year. A visit to the Armenian island, San Lazzaro degli Armeni, makes an absorbing afternoon's round-trip.

SAN GIORGIO MAGGIORE

Daily: May–Sept Mon–Sat 9.30am–6.30pm, Sun 8.30–11am & 2.30–6.30pm; Oct–April closes at dusk. MAP PP.134–135, POCKET MAP J8

Palladio's church of San Giorgio Maggiore, facing the Palazzo Ducale across the Bacino di San Marco, is one of the most prominent and familiar of all Venetian landmarks. It is a startling building, both on the outside and inside, where white stucco is used to dazzling effect – "Of all the colours, none is more proper for churches than white; since the purity of colour, as of the life, is particularly gratifying to God", wrote Palladio. Two outstanding

SAN GIORGIO MAGGIORE

Flooding and the barrier

Called the **acqua alta** (high water), the winter flooding of Venice is caused by a combination of seasonal tides, fluctuations in atmospheric pressure in the Adriatic and persistent southeasterly winds, and has always been a feature of Venetian life. In recent years, though, they have been getting worse: between 2000 and 2013 there were eight highest-category floods, which is more than in the preceeding fifty years – though none was quite as bad as the notorious flood of November 4, 1966, when for 48 hours the sea level remained an average of almost two metres above the mean high tide.

The prospect of global warming and rising sea levels has led to a widespread acceptance of the idea of installing a tidal barrier across the three entrances to the lagoon. Nicknamed **Moisè** (Moses) after the Old Testament's great divider of the waters, this barrier will comprise 79 300-tonne steel flaps, which will lie on the floor of the lagoon; when the water rises to dangerous levels, air will be pumped into the flaps and the barrier will then float upright. In April 2003, more than twenty years after the first plan for Moisè was submitted to the government, Silvio Berlusconi attended a ceremony in Venice to mark the start of work, which is planned for completion in 2017. In the meantime, a host of less extravagant flood-prevention projects has been making progress, with embankments and pavements being rebuilt and raised at numerous flood-prone points, and the 60km of the lagoon's outer coastline being reinforced with stone groynes and artificial reefs to dissipate the energy of the waves.

pictures by **Tintoretto** hang in the chancel: *The Last Supper*, perhaps the most famous of all his works, and *The Fall of Manna*. They were painted as a pair in 1592–94 – the last two years of the artist's life, and a *Deposition* of the same date is in the Cappella dei Morti (visitable only on a €6 guided tour). The door on the left of the choir leads to the **campanile** (€6), the best vantage point in Venice.

The adjoining monastery – now occupied by the **Fondazione Giorgio Cini**, which runs various arts institutes, a naval college and a craft school – is one of the city's architectural wonders, featuring two beautiful cloisters and a magnificent refectory by Palladio. Exhibitions are regularly held here.

GONDOLIER, WITH LA GIUDECCA IN THE BACKGROUND

La Giudecca and San Giorgio Maggiore

LA GIUDECCA

MAP ABOVE, POCKET MAP B8–H9

In the earliest records of Venice the chain of islets now called La Giudecca was known as Spina Longa, a name clearly derived from its shape. The modern name might refer to the Jews (*Giudei*) who lived here from the late thirteenth century until their removal to the Ghetto, but is most likely to originate with the two disruptive noble families who in the ninth century were shoved into this district to keep them out of mischief (*giudicati* means "judged"). Giudecca grew into the city's **industrial** inner suburb: Venice's public transport boats used to be made here; an asphalt factory and a distillery were once neighbours at the western end; and the matting industry, originating in the nineteenth century, kept going

VIEW FROM LA GIUDECCA

here until 1950. However, the semi-dereliction of the present-day island is a potent emblem of Venice's loss of economic self-sufficiency. Swathes of La Giudecca are now purely residential areas, but in this respect things are looking up, with a spate of housing developments and ancillary social facilities being funded in recent years. In no other part of Venice are you as likely to see a site occupied by cranes and bulldozers.

The first vaporetto stop after San Giorgio Maggiore is close to the tiny church of the **Zitelle** (open for Mass only, Sun 10am–noon), which was built in 1582–86 from plans worked out some years earlier by Palladio, albeit for a different site.

At the far end of the island looms the colossal **Mulino Stucky**. With the development of the industrial sector at Marghera (on the mainland) after World War I, the Stucky flour mill went into a nose dive, and in 1954 it closed. As has happened with so many of Venice's prime pieces of real estate, it's now been converted into a hotel and conference centre, in this case by Hilton.

IL REDENTORE

Mon–Sat 10am–5pm. €3 or Chorus Pass
MAP ABOVE, POCKET MAP F9

La Giudecca's main monument, beyond the tug-boats' mooring and the youth hostel (once a granary), is the Franciscan church of Il Redentore, designed by **Palladio** in 1577. In 1575–76 Venice suffered an outbreak of plague that killed nearly fifty thousand people – virtually a third of the city's population. The Redentore was built by the Senate in thanks for Venice's deliverance, and every year until the downfall of the Republic the doge and his senators attended a Mass here to renew their declaration of gratitude, walking to the church over a pontoon bridge from the Záttere. This is the most sophisticated of Palladio's churches, but an appreciation of its subtleties is difficult, as a rope prevents visitors going beyond the nave. In the side chapels you'll find a couple of pictures by Francesco Bassano and an *Ascension* by Tintoretto and his assistants, but the best paintings – including a *John the Baptist* by Jacopo Bassano and a *Baptism of Christ* by Paolo Veronese – are in the sacristy, which is rarely opened.

THE LIDO

The Lido was an unspoilt strip of land until the latter part of the nineteenth century. Byron used to gallop his horses across its fields every day, and as late as 1869 Henry James could describe the island as "a very natural place". Before the century was out, however, it had become the smartest **bathing resort** in Italy, and although it's no longer as chic as it was, there's little room on its beaches in high season. The central stretch of sand used to be, in effect, the preserve of guests at the five-star hotels overlooking it, but a recent test case established that free access must be granted to all; you may, nonetheless, feel more welcome on the less groomed **public beaches** at the northern and southern ends of the island.

In the vicinity of the Piazzale only the **Fortezza di Sant'Andrea** is of much interest, and you have to admire it from a distance across the water – you get a good view from the church and Franciscan monastery of **San Nicolò**. Founded in 1044, when there wasn't so much as a brick wall in this area, the church is notable for its splendid seventeenth-century choir stalls and a few scraps of mosaic that have survived from the eleventh-century building. A stroll along the nearby Via Cipro will bring you to the entrance to Venice's **Jewish cemetery** (guided tours in English May–Oct 2nd & 4th Sun of month 3.30pm; €8.50; reservations at Museo Ebraico or phone ☎041 715 359), which was founded in 1386 and in places has fallen into eloquent decay.

SAN LAZZARO DEGLI ARMENI

Tours daily June–Sept 3pm, Oct–May 3.25pm; €6; the connecting #20 boat leaves San Zaccaria fifteen minutes before the tour starts and returns within ten minutes of the end.

No foreign community has a longer pedigree in Venice than the Armenians, whose presence is most conspicuously signalled by the island of San Lazzaro degli Armeni, identifiable from the city by the onion-shaped summit of its campanile. Tours are conducted by one of the priests who live in the island's **monastery**, and you can expect him to be trilingual, at the very least. Reflecting the encyclopedic interests of its occupants, the monastery is in places like a whimsically arranged museum: at one end of the old **library**, for example, a mummified Egyptian body is laid out near the sarcophagus in which it was found, while at the other is a teak and ivory throne that once seated the governor of Delhi. The monastery's collection of precious manuscripts and books – the former going back to the fifth century – is another highlight of the visit, occupying a modern rotunda in the heart of the complex. Elsewhere you'll see antique metalwork, extraordinarily intricate Chinese ivory carvings, a gallery of works by Armenian artists, a ceiling panel by the young Giambattista Tiepolo, and Canova's figure of Napoleon's infant son, which sits in the chamber in which Byron studied while lending a hand with the preparation of an Armenian–English dictionary. If you're looking for an unusual present, you could buy something at the shop: the old maps and prints of Venice are a bargain.

Restaurants

AL STORICO DA CREA

Imbarcadero del Redentore 212, Giudecca
☎ 041 296 0373. Tues–Sun noon–4pm &
6.30–10pm. MAP PP. 134–135.

Occupying light and airy upper-floor premises in the farthest reaches of Giudecca's biggest boatyard, this cheerful and good-value trattoria is all about fresh fish and seafood, and is popular with locals as well as tourists. For a fantastic view of the southern lagoon, make sure that you reserve a table at the top of the steps. You'll pay around €35–40 per person, with wine.

ALLA PALANCA

Fondamenta Ponte Piccolo 448, Giudecca
☎ 041 528 7719. Mon–Sat 7am–8.30pm.
MAP PP.134–135. POCKET MAP E9

Basic bar-trattoria, but the view of the city from the outside tables is the real appeal. Lunch is served from midday to 2.30pm; before and after lunch, *Alla Palanca* is one of the busiest bars in the Giudecca.

ALLA PALANCA

DA SANDRO

Calle Michelangelo 53c, Giudecca ☎ 041 520
0119. Tues–Sun 10am–3pm & 6–11pm.
MAP PP.134–135. POCKET MAP G9

Recently relocated from its original site amid the Giudecca boatyards, the *osteria* formly known as *Mistrà* retains a canteen-like atmosphere and solid local following, though most of the regulars use it as a bar rather than a restaurant; the menu is strong on fish and seafood, but there's a lot of beef here too, with mains around €20. For the cost-conscious, they do pizzas too, and the new location has a small garden.

CAFÉ AND PEOPLE ON THE LIDO

ACCOMMODATION

Hotels and locande

Venice has well in excess of two hundred hotels, ranging from spartan one-star joints to five-star establishments charging way over €1500 for the best double room in high season. We've indicated the minimum and maximum price for a standard double room; in high season prices will be at the higher end of the scale – though online offers are common. Always bear in mind that you pay through the nose for proximity to the Piazza. In addition, Venice has dozens of private houses offering bed and breakfast (see p.144), as well as *locande*, small family-run establishments with a standard of accommodation equivalent to three- or even four-star hotels (24-hour room service is just about the only facility they don't provide), but often at considerably lower cost. Note, however, that the label *locanda* is used by some upmarket hotels to give them a more homely image.

San Marco: North of the Piazza

AI DO MORI > Calle Larga San Marzo 658 ☎ 041 520 4817, Ⓦ hotelaidomori.com. MAP PP.46–47, POCKET MAP G14. Very friendly, and just a few paces off the Piazza, this is a top recommendation for budget travellers. The top-floor room has a private terrace looking over the Basilica, and is one of the most attractive one-star rooms in the city. €70–150

AL GAMBERO > Calle dei Fabbri 4687 ☎ 041 522 4384, Ⓦ locandaalgambero.com. MAP PP.46–47, POCKET MAP F13. Three-star hotel in an excellent position a short distance off the north side of the Piazza; many of the 26 rooms overlook a canal that's on the standard gondola route from the Bacino Orseolo. There's a popular restaurant on the ground floor. €120–260

CASA PETRARCA > Calle delle Schiavini 4386 ☎ 041 520 0430, Ⓦ casapetrarca.com. MAP PP.46–47, POCKET MAP F14. A very hospitable one-star, one of the cheapest hotels within a stone's throw of the Piazza – but make sure you book well in advance, as it only has seven rooms, including a tiny single. €70–190

ORSEOLO > Corte Zorzi 1083 ☎ 041 520 4827, Ⓦ locandaorseolo .com. MAP PP.46–47, POCKET MAP F14. Superb family-run *locanda* abutting the Orseolo canal, north of the Piazza. Rooms are spacious and light, the breakfasts substantial and the staff hospitable. Entrance is through an iron gate in Campo S. Gallo. €150–260

San Marco: West of the Piazza

ALA > Campo S. Maria del Giglio 2494 ☎ 041 520 8333, Ⓦ hotelalait. MAP PP.52–53, POCKET MAP E15. The 85-room three-star *Ala* – now run by Best Western – has rooms in both modern and traditional Venetian style, and a perfect location on a square that opens out onto the mouth of the Canal Grande. Often has special offers online. €100–200

Booking your accommodation

High season in Venice officially runs from March 15 to November 15 and then from December 21 to January 6, but some places don't recognize the existence of a low season any more. (A few hotels, on the other hand, lower their prices in August when Venice can be hellishly hot and clogged with day-trippers.) During these periods, and Carnevale, it's wise to book at least three months in advance, and for June, July and August it's virtually obligatory to reserve half a year ahead. Bear in mind, also, that many hotels – especially the smaller ones – require you to stay for a minimum of two or three nights in high season.

Online agencies such as W venicehotel.com, W booking.com or W tobook.com can have rooms available in hotels that are nominally full, and may even offer a discount on the hotel's quoted rate. The tourist office's website (W turismovenezia.it) gives details of accommodation of all types. Should you bowl into town with nowhere to stay, you could call in at one of the **AVA/Venezias booking offices**: at the train station (daily: summer 8am–9pm; winter 8am–7pm); on the Tronchetto (9am–8pm); in the multistorey car park at Piazzale Roma (9am–9pm); and at Marco Polo airport (summer 9am–7pm; winter noon–7pm) They only deal with hotels (not hostels or B&Bs) and take a deposit that's deductible from your first night's bill.

ART DECO > Calle delle Botteghe 2966 ☎ 041 277 0558, W locandaartdeco .com. MAP PP.52–53, POCKET MAP D15. This cosy *locanda* has a seventeenth-century palazzo setting, but the interior features 1930s and 40s objects and the pristinely white bedrooms have modern wrought-iron furniture. €90–210

FIORITA > Campiello Nuovo 3457 ☎ 041 523 4754, W locandafiorita .com. MAP PP.52–53, POCKET MAP D14. Welcoming one-star with just ten rooms, so it's crucial to book well ahead. Rooms are all en suite and decorated in eighteenth-century style, and many are spacious. €80–180

FLORA > Calle dei Bergamaschi, off Calle Larga XXII Marzo 2283/a ☎ 041 520 5844, W hotelflora.it. MAP PP.52–53, POCKET MAP E15. This large three-star is very close to the Piazza and has a delightful inner garden. Rooms are beautifully decorated with period pieces, though some are a little cramped. €130–220

KETTE > Piscina S. Moisè 2053 ☎ 041 520 7766, W www.hotelkette .com. MAP PP.52–53, POCKET MAP E15. A four-star favourite with the upper-bracket tour companies: the rooms are sizeable and luxuriously furnished, and it has a central yet quiet location, in an alleyway parallel to Calle Larga XXII Marzo, near La Fenice. Low season prices are very enticing! €120–310

LA FENICE ET DES ARTISTES > Campiello Fenice 1936 ☎ 041 523 2333, W fenicehotels.it. MAP PP.52–53, POCKET MAP E15. In business for more than a century, and recently refurbished, this seventy-room four-star has long been a favoured hangout of the opera crowd, performers and audience alike. Each room is individually decorated (some are all muted pastels, others are a riot of gold and scarlet) and there's also a small garden that's perfect for breakfast. €140–300

MONACO AND GRAND CANAL > Calle Vallaresso 1325 ☎ 041 520 0211, W hotelmonaco.it. MAP PP.52–53, POCKET MAP F15. The ground-floor rooms on the waterfront side of this famous and gorgeous four-star hotel look over to the Salute and are kitted out in traditional Venetian style, with masses of Murano glass and great swags of brocade. In the annexe – the Palazzo Selvadego – you don't get a waterside view, but the decor is lighter, in a nouveau-Mediterranean style, with plain warm colours. €290–500

NOVECENTO > Calle del Dose 2683 ☎ 041 241 3765, Ⓦ www .locandanovecento.it. MAP PP.52–53, POCKET MAP D15. Intimate and very welcoming *locanda* with nine individually decorated doubles, all with bathrooms. Styling is ethnic eclectic (furnishings from Morocco, Japan, China and Egypt), and there's a small courtyard for breakfast. €160–300

Dorsoduro

ACCADEMIA VILLA MARAVEGE > Fondamenta Bollani 1058 ☎ 041 521 0188, Ⓦ pensione accademia.it. MAP PP.60–61, POCKET MAP B16. Once the Russian embassy, this three-star seventeenth-century villa has a devoted following, not least on account of its garden, which occupies a promontory at the convergence of two canals, with a view of a small section of the Canal Grande. Decor is traditional Venetian antique, with bare stone and wooden flooring. Book at least three months ahead. €170–320

AGLI ALBORETTI > Rio Terrà Foscarini 884 ☎ 041 523 0058, Ⓦ aglialboretti .com. MAP PP.60–61, POCKET MAP C16. Friendly and very popular family-run three-star, well situated right next to the Accademia. Its high-season prices compare very favourably with those of many rivals. €120–220

AMERICAN DINESEN > Fondamenta Bragadin 628 ☎ 041 520 4733, Ⓦ hotelamerican.com. MAP PP.60–61, POCKET MAP C16. Nicely located, well-refurbished and welcoming three-star, with some rooms overlooking the Rio di San Vio, a couple of minutes' stroll from the Accademia. €170–310

CA' MARIA ADELE > Rio Terrà dei Catecumeni 111 ☎ 041 520 3078, Ⓦ camariaadele.it. MAP PP.60–61, POCKET MAP F7. Five of the twelve rooms in this very upmarket *locanda* are so-called "theme rooms" – the Sala Noir, for example, is a "voluptuous and hot" environment in cocoa and spice tones. The other rooms are less artfully conceived (and cheaper), but all are spacious and

very comfortable. The adjacent two-room B&B, *Palazzetto 113*, is similarly sybaritic, and similarly priced. €250–550.

CA' PISANI > Rio Terrà Foscarini 979a ☎ 041 240 1411, Ⓦ capisanihotel .it. MAP PP.60–61, POCKET MAP C16. This very glamorous 29-room four-star, just a few metres from the Accademia, created quite a stir when it opened in 2000, chiefly because of its retro styling. Taking its cue from the 1930s and 40s, the *Ca' Pisani* makes heavy use of dark wood and chrome, a refreshing break from the Renaissance and Rococo tones that tend to prevail in Venice's upmarket hotels. €140–350

DD 724 > Ramo da Mula 724 ☎ 041 277 0262, Ⓦ thecharming house.com. MAP PP.60–61, POCKET MAP H16. In a city awash with nostalgia, the high-grade modernist style of this *locanda*, right by the Guggenheim, is very welcome. Each of the seven rooms is impeccably cool and luxurious – and not a Murano chandelier in sight. The same team runs a couple of other similarly sleek properties: a palazzo by Santa Maria Formosa, containing four suites; and a single apartment close to *DD 724*. €180–320

LA CALCINA > Záttere ai Gesuati 780 ☎ 041 520 6466, Ⓦ lacalcina .com. MAP PP.60–61, POCKET MAP E8. Charismatic three-star hotel in the house where Ruskin wrote much of *The Stones of Venice*. From the more expensive rooms you can gaze across to the Redentore, a church that gave him apoplexy. Each of the 29 rooms is uniquely furnished, but all have parquet floors – unusual in Venice. Its restaurant (see p.72) is good. €170–280

LOCANDA SAN BARNABA > Calle del Traghetto 2785 ☎ 041 241 1233, Ⓦ locanda-sanbarnaba.com. MAP PP.60–61, POCKET MAP B15. Exceptionally pleasant and well-priced three-star hotel right by the Ca' Rezzonico. Well-equipped rooms – some have eighteenth-century frescoes, and one has an enormous family-size bath. €130–190

MESSNER > Rio Terrà dei Catacumeni 216 ☎ 041 522 7443, Ⓦ hotelmessner .it. MAP PP.60–61, POCKET MAP F8.

In an excellent, quiet location close to the Salute vaporetto stop, the two-star *Messner* has modern, smart rooms and is run by friendly staff. Some of the rooms are in an annexe round the corner from the smaller but more appealing main building. €130–190

PAUSANIA > Fondamenta Gherardini 3942 ☎ 041 522 2083, Ⓦ hotelpausania.it. MAP PP.60–61, POCKET MAP A15. This quiet, comfortable and friendly three-star has an excellent location very close to San Barnaba church, just five minutes from the Accademia. Very good low-season offers. €120–270

San Polo and Santa Croce

ALEX > Rio Terrà Frari, San Polo 2606 ☎ 041 523 1341, Ⓦ hotelaloxinvenice .com. MAP PP.76–77, POCKET MAP C13. A longstanding budget travellers' favourite, this one-star has been run by the same family since the 1970s; most of the rooms are large and bright, and those with shared bathroom are astoundingly inexpensive. €60–130

CA' ARCO ANTICO > Calle del Forno, San Polo 1451 ☎ 041 241 1227, Ⓦ arcoanticovenice.com. MAP PP.76–77. POCKET MAP D13. Owners Gianfranco and Marco have done a fine job of making this eight-room *locanda* an attractive mix of traditional and modern. With big rooms, great location and excellent breakfasts (a rarity in itself), *Ca' Arco Antico* offers some of the best budget-range accommodation in the city. €60–170

CA' FAVRETTO-SAN CASSIANO > Calle della Rosa, Santa Croce 2232 ☎ 041 524 1768, Ⓦ sancassiano .it. MAP PP.76–77, POCKET MAP D11. Beautiful four-star with some rooms looking across the Canal Grande towards the Ca' d'Oro. Has very helpful staff, a nice courtyard garden and a grand entrance hall. It was once the home of the nineteenth-century painter Giacomo Favretto, and is fitted out in the style of the period. Discounts for stays of three days or more. €80–280

CA' SAN GIORGIO > Salizada del Fondaco dei Turchi 1725, Santa Croce ☎ 041 275 9177, Ⓦ casangiorgio .com. MAP PP.76–77, POCKET MAP C10. Exposed timber beams and walls of raw brick advertise the age of the Gothic palazzo that's occupied by this fine little *locanda*, while the bedrooms are tastefully and very comfortably furnished in quasi-antique style. The gorgeous top-floor suite has its own rooftop terrace. €110–160

OLTRE IL GIARDINO > Fondamenta Contarini 2542, San Polo ☎ 041 275 0015, Ⓦ www.oltreilgiardino-venezia .com. MAP PP.76–77, POCKET MAP B12. This tranquil villa, formerly owned – briefly – by Alma Mahler, has been converted into an immensely stylish six-room hotel; the bedrooms – replete with antiques and works of art – are beautiful and airy, and there's a gorgeous little garden. €180–250

SALIERI > Fondamenta Minotto, Santa Croce 160 ☎ 041 710 035, Ⓦ www .hotelsalieri.com. MAP PP.76–77, POCKET MAP C5. Plain but exceptionally friendly ten-room, one-star hotel, on a picturesque canalside close to the Tolentini church. Rooms are light and airy, and the best ones (for which you pay a premium) overlook the water. €60–140

STURION > Calle del Sturion, San Polo 679 ☎ 041 523 6243, Ⓦ locandasturion.com. MAP PP.76–77, POCKET MAP E12. This eleven-room, three-star has a very long pedigree – the sign of the sturgeon (*sturion*) appears in Carpaccio's *Miracle of the True Cross at the Rialto Bridge* (in the Accademia). It's on a wonderful site overlooking the Canal Grande at the Rialto, but visitors with mobility difficulties should look elsewhere, as the hotel is at the top of three flights of stairs and has no lift. In low season, the rooms with no canal view are a steal. €70–275

B&Bs

The Italian tourism authorities define a bed and breakfast as an establishment with a maximum of three bedrooms available to paying guests, and a minimum of one shared bathroom for guests' exclusive use. The tourist office has lists of dozens of officially registered B&Bs, and the number is growing with each year. Some of these – as you may expect in a city where you could charge €100 plus for the privilege of sleeping on a mattress in the attic – are not terribly attractive, but others are as good as any mid-range hotel. For full listings of Venice's B&Bs, go to Ⓦ www.turismovenezia.it; Ⓦ www.bed-and-breakfast.it is another useful resource. Three recommended B&Bs are:

CA' ANGELI Calle del Traghetto della Madoneta 1434, San Polo ☎ 041 523 2480, Ⓦ caangeli.it. MAP PP.76–77, POCKET MAP D13. An outstanding B&B, very close to Campo San Polo. The owners couldn't be more helpful, the doubles are comfortable and airy, and there's a lovely suite that looks out on the Canal Grande. €100–210

DOMUS ORSONI Calle dei Vedei 1045, Cannaregio ☎ 041 275 9538, Ⓦ domusorsoni.it. MAP PP.88–89, POCKET MAP C2. This unusual B&B, located close to the main Cannaregio canal, is attached to the Orsoni factory, which still manufactures glass mosaics. Each of the five smartly spartan rooms is adorned with a large Orsoni mosaic, and has a mosaic-tiled bathroom. €100–250

FUJIYAMA Calle Lunga San Barnabà 2727a, Dorsoduro ☎ 041 724 1042, Ⓦ bedandbreakfast-fujiyama.it. MAP PP.60–61, POCKET MAP A15. Carlo and Wenyu, the owners of this immaculate B&B, are perfect hosts, and have fitted out their rooms in Japanese/Chinese-inflected style. And this is perhaps the only B&B in Venice that serves real tea – breakfast is taken in the little garden. €75–160

Cannaregio

ABBAZIA > Calle Priuli detta dei Cavalletti 68 ☎ 041 717 333, Ⓦ abbaziahotel.com. MAP PP.88–89, POCKET MAP C3. One of Cannaregio's most restful hotels, the *Abbazia* occupies a former Carmelite monastery (the monks attached to the Scalzi still live in a building adjoining the hotel) and provides three-star amenities without losing its air of quasi-monastic austerity. There's a delightful garden too, and the staff are exceptionally helpful. €90–220

AL PONTE ANTICO > Calle dell'Aseo 5768 ☎ 041 241 1944, Ⓦ alponteantico.com. MAP PP.88–89, POCKET MAP F12. This extremely plush four-star *residenza*, a few metres upstream of the Rialto Bridge, is one of the best small hotels in the city. Decorated throughout in eighteenth-century style, with lashings of gold and blue satin in the bedrooms, it has four grades of accommodation – the "Classic" rooms, which are the simplest, are as good as the best rooms at many pricy Venetian hotels, while the "Deluxe" have huge windows that open onto the Canal Grande. Exceptionally nice staff, too. €220–330

ANTICO DOGE > Sottoportego Falier 5670 ☎ 041 241 1570, Ⓦ anticodoge.com. MAP PP.88–89, POCKET MAP F11. Located within a stone's throw of the church of Santi Apostoli, this very comfortable seven-room three-star hotel occupies part of the palace that once belonged to the disgraced doge Marin Falier. €100–180

BERNARDI SEMENZATO > Calle dell'Oca 4366 ☎ 041 522 7257, Ⓦ hotelbernardi.com. MAP PP.88–89, POCKET MAP F10. Very well-priced two-star hidden in a tiny alleyway close to Campo S. Apostoli, with immensely helpful owners who speak excellent English. Has singles for as little as €40 (with shared bathroom). €70–110

GIORGIONE > Calle Larga dei Proverbi 4587 ☎ 041 522 5810, ⓦ hotelgiorgione.com. MAP PP.88–89, POCKET MAP F10. This plush four-star, very close to Santi Apostoli, has a more personal touch than many of the city's upmarket hotels – it has been run by the same family for many generations. Amenities include a quiet garden and a pool table, and some of the 76 well-equipped rooms have a small private terrace. €80–240

LOCANDA AI SANTI APOSTOLI > Strada Nova 4391a ☎ 041 521 2612, ⓦ locandasantiapostoli.com. MAP PP.88–89, POCKET MAP F11. Occupying the top floor of an ancient palazzo opposite the Rialto market, this ten-room three-star has two lovely rooms overlooking the Canal Grande – for which you'll pay a lot extra. The staff are very helpful, and the location terrific. €100–170

LOCANDA DI ORSARIA > Calle Priuli dei Cavalletti 103 ☎ 041 715 254, ⓦ locandaorsaria.com. MAP PP.88–89, POCKET MAP C3. Though it's situated close to the train station, this very well-managed eight-room *locanda* is nonetheless perfectly quiet; all rooms are en suite and a/c, and larger than is standard at this end of the price scale. €80–200

LOCANDA LEON BIANCO > Corte Leon Bianco 5629 ☎ 041 523 3572, ⓦ leonbianco.it. MAP PP.88–89, POCKET MAP F11. Friendly and charming three-star, tucked away beside the crumbling old Ca' da Mosto, not far from the Rialto Bridge. Only eight rooms, but three of them overlook the Canal Grande (for which there's a premium, of course) and most of the others are spacious and tastefully furnished in eighteenth-century style – one even has a huge Tiepolo-esque fresco. €80–160

NOVO > Calle dei Preti 4529 ☎ 041 241 1496, ⓦ locandanovo .it. MAP PP.88–89, POCKET MAP F11. Basic but popular *locanda* in a refurbished palazzo near Santi Apostoli. The decor might not be to all tastes (there's a lot of pink and orange around the place), and it's quite a haul up four flights of stairs, but most of the rooms are large, and offer very good value for money. €110–170

PALAZZO ABADESSA > Calle Priuli 4011 ☎ 041 241 3784, ⓦ abadessa .com. MAP PP.88–89, POCKET MAP F10. This gorgeous *residenza d'epoca* is a meticulously restored palazzo behind the church of Santa Sofia; all fifteen bedrooms (some of them huge) are nicely furnished with genuine antiques, and there's a lovely secluded garden as well. €110–300

VILLA ROSA > Calle della Misericordia 389 ☎ 041 718 976, ⓦ villarosahotel.com. MAP PP.88–89, POCKET MAP C3. This 31-room two-star is very close to the train station, but nonetheless quiet; the rooms have a/c and private bathrooms, and are bigger than most in this category – the best even have a small balcony. There is a large terrace at the back for breakfast. €90–140

Central Castello

AL LEON > Campo SS. Filippo e Giacomo 4270 ☎ 041 277 0393, ⓦ hotelalleon.com. MAP P.102, POCKET MAP H14. A plain but friendly *locanda*, very close to the Piazza, with eleven pleasantly furnished a/c rooms – not big, but all en suite. €90–140

CANEVA > Corte Rubbi 5515 ☎ 041 522 8118, ⓦ hotelcaneva .com. MAP P.102, POCKET MAP G13. A spartan but well-managed, peaceful and very inexpensive one-star hotel tucked away behind the church of Santa Maria della Fava, close to Campo S. Bartolomeo. Most of the 23 rooms have a/c as well as private bathrooms. €60–140

CASA QUERINI > Campo S. Giovanni Novo 4388 ☎ 041 241 1294, ⓦ www .locandaquerini.com. MAP P.102, POCKET MAP H13. Friendly *locanda* in a quiet courtyard near the Piazza, with six smallish but nicely furnished a/c rooms. €90–160

CASA VERARDO > Calle della Chiesa 4765 ☎ 041 528 6127, ⓦ casaverardo .it. MAP P.102, POCKET MAP H13. A fine three-star hotel occupying a nicely refurbished sixteenth-century palazzo between San Marco and Campo Santa Maria Formosa. Twenty-three well-equipped rooms with a breakfast terrace downstairs, a small garden, a sun lounge at the top and another terrace attached to the priciest of the rooms. €100–250

DANIELI > Riva degli Schiavoni 4196 ☎ 041 522 6480, ⓦ danielihotelvenice .com. MAP P.102, POCKET MAP H14. No longer the most expensive hotel in Venice, but no other place can compete with the glamour of the *Danieli*. Balzac stayed here, as did George Sand, Wagner and Dickens. This magnificent Gothic palazzo affords one of the most sybaritic hotel experiences on the continent – provided you book a room in the old part of the building, not the modern extension. Rooms with a lagoon view are about €150 more expensive than standard doubles. €330–450

DONI > Fondamenta del Vin 4656 ☎ 041 522 4267, ⓦ albergodoni.it.

MAP P.102, POCKET MAP H14. A plain but cosy one-star near San Zaccaria, run by the Doni family since 1946. Most of the thirteen rooms look over the Rio del Vin or a courtyard, but only a few have a private bathroom. €70–130

PAGANELLI > Riva degli Schiavoni 4687 ☎ 041 522 4324, ⓦ hotelpaganelli.com. MAP P.102, POCKET MAP J6. Extensively refitted quite recently, this three-star is a great place to stay, especially if you get one of the rooms on the lagoon side – the ones in the annexe look towards S. Zaccaria, which is a nice enough view, but not quite in the same league. Very good out-of-season rates are available through the website. €90–170

SCANDINAVIA > Campo S. Maria Formosa 5240 ☎ 041 522 3507, ⓦ scandinaviahotel.com. MAP P.102, POCKET MAP H12. Sizeable and comfortable three-star hotel, decorated mainly in eighteenth-century style – lots of Murano glass and floral motifs. Most of the 34 rooms are a decent size, and several of them overlook Campo

Apartments

The very high cost of hotel rooms in Venice makes self-catering an attractive option – for the price of a week in a cramped double room in a three-star hotel you could book yourself a two-bedroom apartment in the centre of the city. The tourist office in Venice has an ever-expanding list of landlords on its books, whose properties (almost three hundred of them, at the last count) can be found through ⓦ turismovenezia.it. The following sites are also worth checking out:

HomeAway ⓦ homeaway.co.uk. This site – which puts you in touch directly with the owners – features hundreds of properties in Venice and the Veneto.

Venetian Apartments ⓦ venice-rentals.com. More than a hundred apartments in the city, ranging from studios at around €1200 per week to an extraordinarily sumptuous palazzo on the Canal Grande at €10,000 a week.

Venice Apartment ⓦ veniceapartment.com. An Italian website with more than 150 properties on its books.

Venice Apartments ⓦ veniceapartments.org. There are dozens of apartments on this well-organized site.

Views on Venice ⓦ viewsonvenice.com. Well-established company with some eighty apartments, and very good service on the ground.

Visit Venice ⓦ visitvenice.co.uk. Two meticulously maintained apartments and a small house, all in Cannaregio; remarkably good value.

Santa Maria Formosa, one of the city's liveliest and best-looking squares. €90–220

Eastern Castello

GABRIELLI > Riva degli Schiavoni 4110 ☎ 041 523 1580, 🌐 hotelgabrielli .it. MAP P.111, POCKET MAP K6. Occupying a beautifully converted Gothic palace, the *Gabrielli* offers four-star comforts and *Danieli*-style views across the Bacino di San Marco for a fraction of the price of the *Danieli*. It also has an attractive little courtyard and a lovely small garden – a rarity in Venice. The website regularly has excellent special offers, such as a lagoon-view double, in high season, for under €300. €160–350

LA RESIDENZA > Campo Bandiera e Moro 3608 ☎ 041 528 5315, 🌐 venicelaresidenza.com. MAP P.111, POCKET MAP K6. This fourteenth-century palazzo is a low-budget gem (in Venetian terms), occupying much of one side of a quiet square just off the main waterfront. It was once a tad pricier than the average two-star, but the rest of the pack have raised their tariffs far more in recent years, making *La Residenza* a top choice. The recently refurbished rooms are elegant and unusually large. €100–200

Hostels

DOMUS CIVICA > Calle Campazzo, San Polo 3082 ☎ 041 771 103, MAP PP.76–77, POCKET MAP A12. This Catholic women's student hostel is open to tourists from mid-June to mid-September. Most rooms are double with running water; showers free; no breakfast; midnight curfew. Very basic, but central and inexpensive: there are discounts if you're staying for a week or more. **Students €25–30 per person, non-students €32–38**

FORESTERIA VALDESE > S. Maria Formosa, Castello 5170 ☎ 041 528 6797, 🌐 www.foresteriavenezia.it. MAP P.102, POCKET MAP H12. Run by Waldensians, this hostel is installed in a wonderful palazzo at the end of Calle Lunga S. Maria Formosa, with flaking frescoes in the rooms and a large communal salon. It has bedrooms for one to four people and small dormitories that can accommodate up to nine; most of the smaller rooms have a private bathroom. Registration 9am–1pm & 6–8pm. Breakfast included. **Doubles from €115, dorms from €32**

OSTELLO SANTA FOSCA > S. Maria dei Servi, Cannaregio 2372, ☎ 041 715 775, 🌐 www.santafosca .com. MAP PP.88–89, POCKET MAP E2. Student-run hostel in an atmospheric former Servite convent in a quiet part of Cannaregio, with rudimentary bedrooms sleeping two to seven people (the larger rooms are female-only), nearly all of them with shared bathrooms. 12.30pm curfew. **Dorms from €27**

OSTELLO VENEZIA > Fondamenta delle Zitelle, Giudecca 86 ☎ 041 523 8211, 🌐 ostellovenezia.it. MAP PP.134–135, POCKET MAP G9. The city's 240-bed, 29-room HI hostel occupies a superb location looking over the water to San Marco, and has recently been completely revamped, making it one of the best in Italy – bright, spacious, comfortable and even stylish. Management once had a reputation for curtness – this too is a thing of the past. Rooms range from doubles to 16-bed mini-dorms. Breakfast and sheets included in the price – but remember to add the expense of the boat from central Venice. No kitchen, but you can eat cheaply in the hostel canteen. No curfew either. Breakfast included. **Dorms €32–36, doubles €130–160**

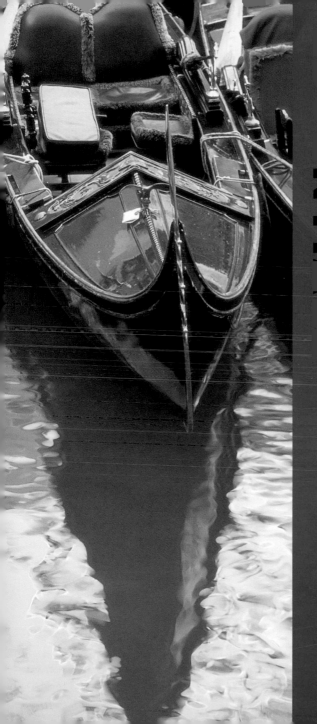

Arrival

Marco Polo airport

Most scheduled flights and some charters arrive at Marco Polo (☎ 041 260 9260, ⊛ www .veniceairport.com), around 7km north of Venice, on the edge of the lagoon. The most inexpensive way into town is to take one of the two road-going **bus services** to the terminal at Piazzale Roma: the ATVO (Azienda Trasporti Veneto Orientale; ⊛ atvo.it) coach, which departs every half-hour and takes around twenty minutes (€6), or the ACTV (Azienda del Consorzio Trasporti Veneziano; ⊛ actv.it) bus #5, which is equally frequent, usually takes just five minutes longer (it's a local bus service, so it picks up and puts down passengers between the airport and Piazzale Roma), and costs €6.

If you'd prefer to approach the city by water, you could take one of the Alilaguna **water-buses**, which operate on three routes from the airport: the Blu line, via Murano, Fondamente Nove, Lido, San Zaccaria, San Marco, Záttere, Giudecca and Terminal Crociere (the docks); the Arancia (Orange), via Madonna dell'Orto, Guglie, San Stae, Rialto, Sant'Angelo, Ca' Rezzonico and San Marco; and the Rosso (Red), via Murano to the Lido (April–Oct). The fare is €15 to any stop in central Venice, and €8 to Murano. All services are hourly, and the journey time to San Marco is about 70min. **Ticket offices** for Alilaguna, ACTV and ATVO services are in the arrivals hall; in addition to single tickets, you can also get ACTV passes here (see p.155) – a wise investment for almost all visitors. Note that ACTV passes are not valid on the Alilaguna service nor on the ATVO bus.

The most luxurious mode of transport is a **water-taxi**. The drivers tout for business in and around the arrivals hall, and will charge in the region of €100 to San Marco for up to six people. Ordinary **car-taxis** cost about €35 to Piazzale Roma.

Treviso airport

Treviso airport is used chiefly by **charter** companies, some of which provide a free bus link from the airport into Venice. An ATVO bus service to Venice's Piazzale Roma meets the incoming Ryanair flights; the fare is €10 single and the journey takes 1 hour 10 minutes. Much quicker are the Barzi buses that run 10–15 times daily from Treviso airport to Piazzale Roma – also costing €10, they take just 40 minutes.

By road and rail

Arriving by **train**, **coach or bus**, you simply get off at the end of the line. The **Piazzale Roma** bus station and **Santa Lucia** train station (don't get off at Venezia Mestre, which is the last stop on the mainland) are just five minutes' walk from each other at the top of the Canal Grande. For details of **left-luggage** facilities, see p.154.

Getting around

With the exceptions of the #1, #2 and the night service, the water-buses skirt the city centre, connecting points on the periphery and the outer islands. Taking a water-bus is usually the quickest way of getting between far-flung points, but in many cases the speediest way of getting from A to B is on foot – you don't have to run, for instance, to cover the distance from the Piazza to the Rialto Bridge more quickly than the #1 boat. Once you've got your bearings navigation is not as daunting as it seems at first. Yellow signs posted high up on streetcorners all over central Venice indicate the main routes to San Marco, Ferrovia (train station) and Rialto. For public transport enquiries ACTV have an office at Piazzale Roma (daily 7.30am–8pm); or ⓦ actv.it.

Water-buses

There are two types of water-bus: the **vaporetti**, which are the workhorses used on the Canal Grande services (#1 and #2) and other heavily used routes; and the smaller **motoscafi**, which are employed on routes where the volume of traffic isn't as great (notably the two "circular routes" – #4.1/4.2 and #5.1/5.2).

The standard **fare** is an exorbitant €7 for a single journey; the ticket is valid for sixty minutes, and for any number of changes of waterbus, but cannot be used as a return ticket. There's a €4 ticket for one-stop hops across the Canal Grande, or between San Zaccaria and San Giorgio Maggiore, or the Lido and Sant'Elena. If you have more than one piece of large luggage, you're supposed to pay €7 per additional item. Children under 4 travel free on all water-buses. **Tickets** are available from most landing stages, shops displaying the ACTV sign, and all the tourist offices; the travel passes are available from the tourist offices and at the Piazzale Roma, train station, Ca' d'Oro, Rialto, Accademia, San Marco Vallaresso, San Zaccaria, Arsenale, Záttere, Fondamente Nove and Tronchetto vaporetto stops. In the remoter parts of the city you may not be able to find anywhere to buy a ticket, particularly after

working hours, when the booths at the landing stages tend to close down; tickets can be bought on board at the standard price, as long as you ask the attendant as soon as you get on board; if you delay, you could be liable for a hefty spot-fine.

Unless you intend to walk all day, you'll almost certainly save money by buying some sort of **travel card** as soon as you arrive. ACTV produces tickets valid for **24 hours** (€20), **48 hours** (€30), **72 hours** (€40), and **seven days** (€60), which can be used on all ACTV services within Venice. A supplement of €4 per journey is payable if you want to use an ACTV pass on the airport buses.

All tickets and travel passes must be **validated** before embarking, by swiping the card across one of the machines at the entrance to the vaporetto stop; you need to swipe it just once. Even if your travel pass is valid you'll still be fined if you haven't swiped it before getting aboard.

Water-bus routes

What follows is a run-through of the water-bus routes that visitors are most likely to find useful; a full **timetable** can be downloaded from ⓦactv.it and can usually be picked up at the Piazzale Roma, Ferrovia, San Marco, San Zaccaria, Accademia and Fondamente Nove vaporetto stops.

Be warned that so many services call at **San Marco**, **San Zaccaria**, **Rialto** (scene of a fatal collision between a vaporetto and a gondola in 2013) and the **train station** that the stops at these points are spread out over a long stretch of waterfront, so you might have to walk past several stops before finding the one you need. Note that the main San Marco stop is also known as **San Marco Vallaresso**, or plain Vallaresso, and that the San Zaccaria stop is as close to the Basilica as is the Vallaresso stop.

#1

The slowest of the water-buses, and the one you'll use most often. It starts at Piazzale Roma, calls at every stop on the **Canal Grande** except San Samuele, works its way along the **San Marco** waterfront to **Sant'Elena**, then goes over to the **Lido**. The #1 runs every 20min 5–6.30am, every 10min 6.30am–10pm and every 20min 10–11.40pm. For the night service, see #N.

#2

The timetable of the #2 is immensely complicated, but basically from around 9am to 5pm its clockwise route takes it from San Zaccaria to San Giorgio Maggiore, Giudecca (Zitelle, Redentore and Palanca), Záttere, San Basilio, Sacca Fisola, Tronchetto, Piazzale Roma, the train station, then down the Canal Grande (calling only at Rialto, San Tomà, San Samuele and Accademia) to San Marco Giardinetti; the anti-clockwise version calls at the same stops. It runs in both directions every 12min. From around 5–9am and 5–11.30pm, however, the lower section of Canal Grande is omitted, so the #2 runs back and forth between San Zaccaria and Rialto, every 20min. In summer the #2 is extended out to the Lido, via Giardini.

#4.1/4.2

The **circular service**, running right round the core of Venice, with a short detour at the northern end to **San Michele** and **Murano**. The #4.1 travels anticlockwise, the #4.2 clockwise and both run every 20min

7am–8.30pm; before and after that, the #4.1/4.2 together act as a shuttle service between Murano and Fondamente Nove, running every 20min from 4.30am until around 11.30pm.

#5.1/5.2

Similar to the #4.1/4.2, this route also **circles Venice**, but heads out to the **Lido** (rather than Murano) at the easternmost end of the circle. The #5.1 runs anticlockwise, the #5.2 clockwise, and both run fast through the Giudecca canal, stopping only at Záttere and Santa Marta between San Zaccaria and Piazzale Roma. Be aware that in the early morning and late evening neither service does a complete loop of the city.

#12

For most of the day, from 4.30am, the **#12** runs every half hour from Fondamente Nove (approximately hourly 7.40–11pm), calling first at **Murano-Faro** before heading on to **Mazzorbo**, **Burano** (from where there is a connecting half-hourly shuttle to Torcello), and Treporti; it runs with the same frequency in the opposite direction.

#3

From around 6am to 6pm the **#3** runs from Tronchetto via Piazzale Roma and Ferrovia to Murano, where it always calls at Colonna and Museo, and often at other Murano stops too.

#N

This **night service** (11.30pm–4.30am) is a selective fusion of the #1 and #2 routes. Another night service connects Venice with Murano and Burano, running to and from Fondamente

Nove every hour between 11.30pm & 3am.

Traghetti

Costing €2 for non-residents, **traghetti** (gondola ferries) are the only cheap way of getting a ride on a gondola, albeit a stripped-down version, with none of the trimmings and no padded seats – most Venetians stand up. The gondola traghetti across the Canal Grande are as follows; in the winter months it's common for services to be suspended.

Campiello del Traghetto (Santa Maria del Giglio) **Calle Lanza** (near the Salute; daily 9am–6pm)

Ca' Rezzonico–San Samuele (Mon–Sat 0.30am–1.30pm)

San Tomà–Sant'Angelo (Mon–Sat 7.30am–8pm, Sun 8.30am–7.30pm)

Riva del Carbon–Fondamenta del Vin (Mon–Sat 8am–1pm)

Santa Sofia–Rialto (Mon–Sat 7.30am–8pm, Sun 8.45am–7pm)

San Marcuola–Fondaco dei Turchi (Mon–Sat 9am–1pm)

Fondamenta Santa Lucia–Fondamenta San Simeon Piccolo (daily 9am–6pm).

Gondolas

The gondola, once Venice's chief form of transport, is now purely an adjunct of the tourist industry. But however much the gondola's image has become tarnished, it is an astonishingly graceful craft, perfectly designed for negotiating the tortuous and shallow waterways, and an hour's slow voyage through the back canals can give you a wholly new perspective on the city.

To hire a gondola costs €80 per forty minutes for up to six passengers, rising to €100 between 7pm and 8am; you pay an extra €40 for every additional twenty minutes, or €50 from 7pm to 8am. Further hefty surcharges will be levied should you require the services of an on-board accordionist or tenor – and a surprising number of people do. Even though the tariff is set by the local authorities, it's been known for gondoliers to extort even higher rates than these – if you do decide to go for a ride, establish the charge before setting off. To minimize the chances of being ripped off by a private individual making a few dozen euros on the side (and there are plenty of those in Venice), take a boat only from one of the following official gondola stands: west of the Piazza at Calle Vallaresso, Campo San Moisè or Campo Santa Maria del Giglio; immediately north of the Piazza at Bacino Orseolo; on the Molo, in front of the Palazzo Ducale; outside the *Danieli* hotel on Riva degli Schiavoni; at the train station; at Piazzale Roma, at Campo Santa Sofia, near Ca' d'Oro; at San Tomà, to the east of the Frari; or by the Rialto Bridge on Riva Carbon.

Taxis

Venice's **water-taxis** are sleek and speedy vehicles that can penetrate all but the shallowest of the city's canals. Unfortunately they are possibly the most expensive form of taxi in Europe: the clock starts at €15 and goes up €2 every minute. All sorts of additional surcharges are levied as well: €10 for each extra person if there are more than five people in the party; €5 for each piece of luggage in excess of five items; €10 for a ride between 10pm & 6am. There are five ways of getting a taxi: go to one of the main stands (at Piazzale Roma, the train station, Rialto and San Marco Vallaresso), find one in the process of disgorging its passengers, call one by phone (☎ 041 522 2303), email at ✉ info@motoscafivenzia.it or book through ✇ www.motoscafivenzia.it.

Directory A–Z

Consulates and embassies

The nearest **British** consulate is in Milan, at Via San Paolo 7 (☎ 02 723 001). The nearest **US** consulate is also in Milan, at Via Principe Amedeo 2-10 (☎ 02 290 351), but there's a consular agency at Marco Polo airport (☎ 041 541 5944). Travellers from **Ireland**, **Australia**, **New Zealand** and **Canada** should contact their Rome embassies: Irish Embassy, Piazza di Campitelli 3 ☎ 06 697 9121; Australian Embassy, Via Alessandria 215 ☎ 041 06 852 721; New Zealand Embassy, Via Clitunno 44 ☎ 06 853 7501; Canadian Embassy, Via Zara 30 ☎ 041 06 444 2911.

Electricity

The supply in Italy is 220V, though anything requiring 240V will work. Most plugs have two round pins: UK equipment will need an adaptor, US equipment a 220-to-110 transformer as well.

Emergencies

For police emergencies ring ☎ 113. Alternatively, dialling ☎ 112 puts you straight through to the *Carabinieri* (military police), ☎ 115 goes straight to the *Vigili del Fuoco* (fire brigade) and ☎ 118 straight to *Pronto Soccorso Medico* (ambulance).

Hospital

Ospedale Civile, Campo SS. Giovanni e Paolo ☎ 041 529 4111.

Internet access

Many hotels and hostels now offer free internet access, and there are internet points (usually charging €6–8 per hour) all over the city, especially in the area around Campo Santa Margherita and Campo San Barnaba. At all of them you'll need to present ID before logging on. Many of these places are short-lived, but you should find the following still in operation:

San Marco: Venetian Navigator, Calle dei Stagneri 5239 (daily: summer 10am–10pm; winter 10am–8.30pm).

Dorsoduro: Terminal Fusina, Rio Terrà dei Gesuati 909c (Mon–Sat 8.30am–1pm); San Barnaba, Campo San Barnaba 2759 (Mon–Sat 7am–7pm).

Cannaregio: Planet Internet, Rio Terà San Leonardo 1519 (daily 9am–11pm); ABColor, Lista di Spagna 220 (daily: summer 10am–10pm, winter 10am–8pm).

Castello: Venetian Navigator, Calle Casselleria 5300 (daily: summer 10am–10pm; winter 10am–8.30pm).

Left luggage

There's a left luggage office at Piazzale Roma (daily 6am–8pm) and another beside platform 1 at the train station (daily 6am–11pm), each costing €6 per item for the first 5hr, then an extra €0.90/hr until the 12hr mark, and €0.40/hr thereafter.

Lost property

If you lose anything on the train or at the station, call ☎ 041 785 531; at the airport call ☎ 041 260 9222; on the water- or land buses call ☎ 041 272 2179; and anywhere in the city itself call ☎ 041 274 8225.

Money

Banks are concentrated around Campo San Luca and Campo Manin (in the north of the San Marco *sestiere*). Hours are generally Mon–Fri 8.30am–1.30pm & 2.30–3.30pm.

There are clusters of exchange bureaux (*cambio*) near San Marco, the Rialto and the train station. Open late every day of the week, they can

The Venezia Unica Tourist Pass & Rolling Venice

For tourists who intend to do some intensive sightseeing, the city has a ludicrously complicated scheme called **Venezia Unica** (ⓦveneziaunica.it), in which you choose a menu of services online (museum passes, waterbuses, wi-fi networks, public toilets etc), and are then quoted a price for a ticket that also includes discounts to some other museums and exhibitions. (The collection process is explained on the website.) Note that there are two versions of the Venezia Unica pass: this one, which is for tourists; and the "frequent users" pass, which is a travel permit for long-stayers. Given that the full-price Venezia Unica pass costs around €40 without the transport option, and that its 7-day period of validity begins when you collect it (whereas ACTV Travel Cards are valid from the moment you first use them), for most visitors it's best just to buy a Travel Card and/or Museum Pass when you arrive in Venice.

If you're aged between 14 and 29, you are eligible for a **Rolling Venice** card, which gives you some discounts at certain shops, restaurants, museums and exhibitions (details are given in a leaflet that comes with the card) and entitles you to a 72-hour ACTV travel pass (not valid for the airport bus) for just €20. The Rolling Venice card costs €4 and is available from the tourist offices, on production of a passport.

---

be useful in emergencies, but their rates of commission and exchange tend to be steep.

Museums and monuments

There are two **Museum Cards** for the city's civic museums (ⓦvisitmuve.it). The **Musei di Piazza San Marco** card costs €17 (€10 for ages 6–14, students under 30, EU citizens over 65 & Rolling Venice Card holders), and gets you into the Palazzo Ducale, Museo Correr, Museo Archeologico and the Biblioteca Marciana; it's valid for three months. The **Museum Pass**, costing €24/18, covers these four, plus all the other civic museums: Ca' Rezzonico, Casa Goldoni, Palazzo Mocenigo, Museo di Storia Naturale, Ca' Pésaro (the modern art and oriental museums), the Museo del Merletto (Burano) and the Museo del Vetro (Murano). It's valid for six months. Both passes allow one visit to each attraction and are available from any of the participating museums. The Palazzo Ducale and Museo Correr can be visited only with a museum card; at the other places you have the option of paying an entry charge just for that attraction. Accompanied disabled people have free access to all civic museums.

Fifteen churches are part of the **Chorus Pass** scheme (ⓦchorus venezia.org), whereby a **€12 ticket** allows one visit to each of the churches over a one-year period. The proceeds from the scheme are ploughed back into the maintenance of the member churches. The individual entrance fee at each church is €3, and all are open to tourists from Monday to Saturday, 10am to 5pm (except where stated otherwise, below). The churches involved are: the Frari (Mon–Sat 9am–6pm, Sun 1–6pm); the Gesuati; the Redentore; San Giacomo dell'Orio; San Giobbe (Mon–Sat 10am–1.15pm); San Giovanni Elemosinario; San Pietro di Castello; San Polo; San Sebastiano; San Stae; Sant'Alvise

(Mon–Sat 1.45–5pm); Santa Maria dei Miracoli; Santa Maria del Giglio; Santa Maria Formosa; Santo Stefano. The Chorus Pass is available at all of these churches, and from the Venice Pavilion tourist office.

Police

To notify police of a theft or lost passport, report to the *Questura*, which is at Rampa Santa Chiara 500, on the north side of the road bridge that leads onto Piazzale Roma (☎041 271 5511). There's a small police station on the Piazza, at no. 63.

Post offices

Venice's central **post office** is at Calle delle Acque 5016, close to San Salvador, and is open Mon–Fri 8.30am–7pm, Sat 8.30am–12.30pm). The principal branch offices are located at Calle dell'Ascensione 1241 (off the west side of the Piazza), Calle del Spezier 233 and Záttere 1507 (both Dorsoduro), Campo San Polo 2012, and Barbaria delle Tole 6674 and Via Garibaldi 1641 (both Castello). Stamps can also be bought in *tabacchi*, as well as in some gift shops.

Public toilets

There are toilets on or very near most of the main squares, signposted by green and white "WC" stickers on the walls or ground. You'll need €1.50, but many toilets are staffed, so you can get change; note that the Venice Card (see p.155) gives free access to staffed toilets. The main facilities are at Piazzale Roma; in the Giardinetti Reali, by the main tourist office; off the west side of the Piazza; the train station; and on the west side of the Accademia bridge.

Telephones

Most of Venice's public call-boxes accept coins, and all of them take phone cards, which can be bought from *tabacchi* and some other shops (look for the Telecom Italia sticker). You're never far from a pay phone – every sizeable campo has at least one, and there are phones by every vaporetto stop. Note that many internet points offer international calls at a better rate than you'll get from Telecom Italia's public phones.

Time

Italy is on Central European Time (CET), which means that it is one hour ahead of the UK, six hours ahead of Eastern Standard Time and nine hours ahead of Pacific Standard Time.

Tourist information

For many years Venice's main **tourist office** has been the Venice Pavilion (otherwise known as the Palazzina del Santi), the waterfront building on the west side of the Giardinetti Reali; when we went to press it was in the throes of a major refurbishment, leaving the office at Calle dell'Ascensione 71/f, in the corner of the Piazza's arcades, as the only office in the centre of the city (daily 8.30am–7pm; ☎041 523 0399; ⊛turismovenezia.it). The Calle dell'Ascensione office is also the main outlet for information on the rest of the Veneto. There are two offices at the train station: one by platform 1, and the other outside the station (both daily 8.30am–7pm). Other offices are in the airport arrivals area (daily 8.30am–8pm) and at the multistorey car park at Piazzale Roma (daily 8.30am–2pm).

For printed information, a useful resource is the English–Italian magazine *Un Ospite di Venezia* (⊛unospitedivenezia.it); it gives information on exhibitions, concerts and events, plus extras such as

Useful websites

ⓦ**churchesofvenice.co.uk** Jeff Cotton's wonderful website is replete with fascinating facts and stories about the churches of Venice, Verona and Padua.

ⓦ**iamnotmakingthisup.net** Erla Zwingle's witty and eye-opening blog on life in Venice.

ⓦ**veneto.to** The official Veneto tourist office site with information on places to visit, hotels, weather, festivals and exhibitions.

ⓦ**veneziablog.blogspot.co.uk** An excellent blog by a Venice-dwelling American–Italian who goes by the name of "Signor Nonloso".

ⓦ**veneziaunica.it** This website is the place to go for info on the Venezia Unica passes, and the city's calendar of events.

ⓦ**turismovenezia.it** The official Venice tourist office site is rather clunky, but it's packed with practical stuff on museums, accommodation and restaurants.

ⓦ**venicetravelblog.com** Durant and Cheryl Imboden's website is a good source of up-to-the-minute practical information for visitors to the city.

ⓦ**venicexplorer.net** This site features hundreds of images, a calendar of daily events, a map search facility and a vast range of information, covering everything from Venetian cuisine to conservation issues.

vaporetto timetables, and is free from the reception desks of many four- and five-star hotels. The fullest source of information, though, is *VENews* (€3; ⓦvenezianews.it), which is published ten times a year and is sold at newsstands all over the city; it has good coverage of exhibitions, cultural events, bars and restaurants, with a fair amount of text in English as well as coverage in Italian.

Festivals and events

CARNEVALE

The ten days before Lent ⓦwww
.carnivalofvenice.com.

John Evelyn wrote of the 1646 Carnevale: "all the world was in Venice to see the folly and madness...the women, men and persons of all conditions disguising themselves in antique dresses, & extravagant Musique & a thousand gambols". Not much is different in today's Carnevale, for which people arrive in such numbers that the causeway from the mainland has sometimes had to be closed because the city is too packed. Originating as a communal party prior to the abstemious rigours of Lent, Carnevale takes place over ten days, finishing on Shrove Tuesday with a masked ball for the glitterati, and dancing in the Piazza for the plebs. During the day people parade in costumes on the Piazza; parents dress up their kids; businessmen can be seen doing their shopping in the classic white mask, black cloak and tricorne hat. In the evening some congregate in the remoter squares, while those in elaborate costumes install themselves in the windows of *Florian*. But you don't necessarily need to spend much money: a simple black outfit and a painted face is enough to transform you from a spectator into a participant.

LA SENSA

May, Sun after Ascension Day

The feast of La Sensa happens on the Sunday after Ascension Day – the latter being the day on which the doge enacted the wedding of Venice to the sea. The ritual has recently been revived – a distinctly feeble procession which ends with the mayor and a gang of other dignitaries getting into a present-day approximation of the *Bucintoro* (the state barge) and sailing off to the Lido. A gondola regatta follows the ceremony.

VOGALONGA

Second Sun after Ascension

Far more spectacular than La Sensa is the Vogalonga ("long row"), which is held a week later. Established in 1974 as a protest against the excessive number of motorboats on the canals, the Vogalonga is now open to any crew in any class of rowing boat, and covers a 32km course from the Bacino di San Marco to Burano and back; the competitors set off at 8.30am and arrive at the bottom of the Canal Grande anywhere between about 11am & 3pm.

THE BIENNALE

June–Nov, odd numbered years
ⓦlabiennale.org.

The Venice Biennale, Europe's most glamorous international forum for contemporary art, was inaugurated in 1895 and is now held every odd-numbered year from June to November. The main site is by the Giardini Pubblici, with permanent pavilions for about forty countries plus space for a thematic international exhibition. This core part is supplemented by exhibitions in parts of the Arsenale that are otherwise closed to the public, such as the colossal Corderie or Tana (the former rope-factory). Various sites throughout the city (eg salt warehouses on the Záttere) are used as national pavilions and as venues for fringe exhibitions. Some of the Biennale pavilions and other buildings (usually the Tana) are used in even-numbered years for an independent Biennale for architecture, a smaller event which runs from the second week of September to mid-November; this overlaps with a brief music Biennale, and is preceded by a two-week dance Biennale.

FESTA DEL REDENTORE

Third Sun in July

The Festa del Redentore is one of Venice's plague-related festivals, marking the end of the 1576 epidemic. The day centres on Palladio's church of the Redentore, which was built by way of thanksgiving. A bridge of boats is strung across the Giudecca canal to allow the faithful to walk over to the church, and on the preceding Saturday night hundreds of people row out for a picnic on the water. The night ends with fireworks, after which it's traditional to row to the Lido for sunrise.

THE FILM FESTIVAL

Eleven days in late Aug and/or early Sept ⓦlabiennale.org.

The Venice Film Festival (Mostra Internazionale d'Arte Cinematografica), founded in 1932, is the world's oldest. The eleven-day event takes place on the Lido. The main screen is the **Palazzo del Cinemà**, next to the *Excelsior* hotel on Lungomare G. Marconi; other screenings take place in the vast **PalaBiennale** marquee, the four-screen **Palazzo del Casinò**, and the **Sala Darsena**. Tickets are available to the public on the day before the performance, at the Palazzo del Cinemà and PalaBiennale ticket offices and at the Biennale HQ, just west of the Piazza at Calle del Ridotto 1365a.

THE REGATA STORICA

First Sun in Sept

The Regata Storica is the annual trial of strength and skill for the city's gondoliers and other expert rowers. It starts with a procession of richly decorated historic craft along the Canal Grande, their crews all decked out in period dress, followed by a series of races right up the canal. Re-enacting the return of Caterina Cornaro to her native city in 1489, the opening parade is spectacular. The first race of the day is for young rowers in two-oared *pupparini*; the women's race comes next (in boats called *mascarete*), followed by a race for canoe-like *caorline*; and then it's the big one – the men's race, in specialized two-man racing gondolas called *gondolini*.

LA SALUTE

Nov 21

The Festa della Salute is a reminder of the 1630–31 plague, which killed one third of the lagoon's population. The Salute church was built in thanks for deliverance from the outbreak, and since then the Venetians have processed over a pontoon bridge across the Canal Grando to give thanks for their health, or to pray for the sick. It offers the only chance to see the church as it was designed to be seen – with its main doors open and hundreds of people milling up and down the steps.

National holidays

Many fee-charging sights (but not bars and restaurants) close on the following dates: **January 1**; **January 6** (Epiphany); **Easter Monday**; **April 25** (Liberation Day and St Mark's Day); **May 1** (Labour Day); **June 2** (Day of the Republic); **August 15** (Assumption of the Blessed Virgin Mary); **November 1** (Ogni Santi, "All Saints"); **December 8** (Immaculate Conception of the Blessed Virgin Mary); **December 25**; **December 26**. Many Venetian shops and businesses also close or work shorter hours for the local festival of the Salute on **November 21**.

Chronology

453 > The first mass migration into the Venetian lagoon is provoked by the incursions of Attila the Hun's hordes.

568 > Permanent settlement is accelerated when the Germanic Lombards (or Longobards) sweep into northern Italy. The resulting confederation owes political allegiance to Byzantium.

726 > The lagoon settlers choose their first doge, Orso Ipato.

810 > After the Frankish army of Charlemagne has overrun the Lombards, the emperor's son Pepin sails into action against the proto-Venetians and is defeated. The lagoon settlers withdraw to the better-protected islands of Rivoalto, the name by which the central cluster of islands was known until the late twelfth century, when it became generally known as Venice.

828 > The Venetians signal their independence through a great symbolic act – the theft of the body of St Mark from Alexandria. St Mark is made the patron saint of the city, and a basilica is built alongside the doge's castle to accommodate the holy relics.

1000 > A fleet commanded by Doge Pietro Orseolo II subjugates the Slav pirates who have been impeding Venetian trade in the northern Adriatic. The expedition is commemorated annually in the ceremony of the Marriage of Venice to the Sea.

1081 > The Byzantine emperor Alexius Comnenus appeals to Venice for aid against the Normans of southern Italy. In the following year the emperor declares Venetian merchants to be exempt from all tolls and taxes within his lands. In the words of one historian – "On that day Venetian world trade began".

1095 > The commencement of the First Crusade. Offering to transport armies and supplies to the East in return for grants of property and financial bonuses, Venice extends its foothold in the Aegean, the Black Sea and Syria.

1177 > Having been embroiled in the political manoeuvrings between the papacy, the Western Emperor and the cities of northern Italy, Venice brings off one of its greatest diplomatic successes: the reconciliation of Emperor Frederick Barbarossa and Pope Alexander III.

1204 > Venice plays a major role in the Fourth Crusade and the Sack of Constantinople. Thousands are massacred by the Christian soldiers and virtually every precious object that can be lifted is stolen from the city, mainly by the Venetians, who now have an almost uninterrupted chain of ports stretching from the lagoon to the Black Sea.

1297 > The passing of the Serrata del Maggior Consiglio, a measure which basically allows a role in the government of the city only to those families already involved in it. The Serrata is to remain in effect, with minimal changes, until the end of the Venetian Republic five centuries later.

1310 > Following an uprising led by Bajamonte Tiepolo, the Council of Ten is created to supervise internal security.

1355 > Doge Marin Falier is executed, after plotting to overthrow the councils of Venice and install himself as absolute ruler.

1380 > Almost a century of sporadic warfare against Genoa – Venice's chief commercial rival in the eastern Mediterranean – climaxes with the War of Chioggia. The invading Genoese are driven out of the lagoon, and it soon becomes clear that Venice has at last won the tussle for economic and political supremacy.

1420 > Venice annexes **Friuli** and **Udine**, which were formerly ruled by the King of Hungary, virtually doubling the area of its *terra firma* (mainland) empire, extending it right up to the Alps.

1441 > Doge Francesco Fóscari, having led Venice against Filippo Maria Visconti of Milan, signs the Treaty of Cremona, which confirms Venetian control of Peschiera, Brescia, Bergamo and part of the territory of Cremona.

1453 > Constantinople falls to the Turkish army of Sultan Mahomet II, which results in the erosion of Venice's commercial empire in the East.

1494 > Italy is invaded by Louis XII of France. In the ensuing chaos Venice succeeds in adding bits and pieces to its *terra firma* domain, but when it begins to encroach on papal territory in Romagna, it provokes – in 1508 – the formation of the League of Cambrai, with Pope Julius II,

Louis XII, Emperor Maximilian and the King of Spain at its head.

1499 > The defeat of the Venetian navy at Sapienza leads to the loss of the main fortresses of the Morea (Peloponnese), which means that the Turks now control the so-called "door to the Adriatic".

1516 > End of the War of the League of Cambrai. Venice still possesses nearly everything it held at the start of the war, but many of the cities of the Veneto have been sacked and the Venetian treasury bled almost dry.

1519 > With the accession of the 19-year-old Charles V, the Habsburg Empire absorbs the massive territories of the Spanish kingdom, and the whole Italian peninsula, with the sole exception of Venice, is soon under the emperor's domination.

1571 > The Venetian fleet is instrumental in the defeat of the Turks at Lépanto, but in subsequent negotiations Venice is forced to surrender Cyprus.

1606 > Friction between the papacy and Venice comes to a head with a Papal Interdict and the excommunication of the whole city.

1669 > Prolonged Turkish harassment of the Venetian colonies culminates with the fall of Crete.

1699 > Under the command of Doge Francesco Morosini, the Venetians embark on a retaliatory action in the Morea (Peloponnese), and succeed in retaking the region, albeit for only a short time.

1718 > In the Treaty of Passarowitz Venice is forced to accept a definition of its Mediterranean empire drawn up by the Austrians and the Turks. It is left with just the Ionian islands and the Dalmatian coast, and its power in these colonies is little more than hypothetical.

1748 > By now a political nonentity, Venice signs the Treaty of Aix-la-Chapelle, which confirms Austrian control of what had once been Venice's mainland empire.

1797 > Having mollified the Austrians by handing over the Veneto to them, Napoleon waits for a pretext to polish off the Republic itself. On April 20, the Venetians attack a French naval patrol off the Lido. On May 9 an ultimatum is sent to the city's government, demanding the dissolution of its constitution. On Friday, May 12, 1797, the Maggior Consiglio (in effect the city's parliament) meets for the last time, voting to accede to Napoleon's demands. The Venetian Republic is dead. By the Treaty of Campo Formio, Napoleon relinquishes Venice to the Austrians.

1805 > Napoleon joins the city to his Kingdom of Italy, and it stays under French domination until the aftermath of Waterloo.

1815 > Venice passes back to the Austrians, and remains a Habsburg province for the next half-century, the only break in Austrian rule coming with the revolt of March 1848, when the city is reinstituted as a republic under the leadership of Daniele

Manin. The rebellion lasts until August 1849.

1866 > Venice is absorbed into the Kingdom of United Italy.

1869 > The opening of the Suez Canal brings a muted revival to the shipbuilders of Venice's Arsenale, but tourism is now emerging as the main area of economic expansion, with the development of the Lido as Europe's most fashionable resort.

1917 > The navy dismantles the Arsenale and switches its yards to Genoa and Naples.

1933 > A road link is built to carry workers between Venice and the steadily expanding refineries and factories of Porto Marghera. Rapid depopulation of the historic centre soon follows, as workers decamp to Marghera's neighbour, Mestre, where housing is drier, roomier, warmer and cheaper.

2003 > With the number of annual *acque alte* (floods) exceeding one hundred, in April 2003 work begins on the construction of the tidal barrier (see p.133).

2008 > The population of the historic centre of Venice falls below sixty thousand. The annual number of tourist visits now exceeds twenty million; tourism generates around seventy percent of the city's income.

2012 > The sixth-worst floods ever recorded hit the city in November.

2014 > The city's mayor is arrested in connection with alleged corruption, relating to the flood barrier.

Italian

What follows is a brief pronunciation guide and a rundown of essential words and phrases. For more detail, see the *Italian: Rough Guide Phrasebook*.

Pronunciation

Italian **pronunciation** is easy, since every word is spoken exactly as it is written, with only a few **consonants** that are different from English:

c before e or i is pronounced as in **ch**urch; **ch** before the same vowels is hard, as in **c**at.

sci or **sce** are pronounced as in **sh**eet and **sh**elter respectively.

g is soft before **e** and **i**, as in **g**eranium; hard when followed by **h**, as in **g**arlic.

gn has the ni sound of our "onion".

gl in Italian is softened to something like li in English, as in stal**li**on.

h is not aspirated, as in **h**onour.

Italian words are stressed on the penultimate syllable unless an accent (´ or `) denotes otherwise, although written accents are often left out in practice. Note that the ending -ia or -ie counts as two syllables, hence *trattoria* is stressed on the **i**.

Words and phrases

BASICS

Good morning	Buon giorno
Good afternoon /evening	Buona sera
Good night	Buona notte
Goodbye	Arrivederci
Yes	Sì
No	No
Please	Per favore
Thank you (very much)	Grázie (molte/mille grazie)
You're welcome	Prego
Alright/that's OK	Va bene
How are you?	Come stai/sta? (informal/formal)
I'm fine	Bene
Do you speak English?	Parla inglese?
I don't understand	Non ho capito
I don't know	Non lo so
Excuse me	Mi scusi/Prego
Excuse me (in a crowd)	Permesso
I'm sorry	Mi dispiace
I'm English	Sono inglese
Scottish	scozzese
American	americano
Irish	irlandese
Welsh	gallese
Today	Oggi
Tomorrow	Domani
Day after tomorrow	Dopodomani
Yesterday	Ieri
Now	Adesso
Later	Più tardi
Wait a minute!	Aspetta!
In the morning	Di mattina
In the afternoon	Nel pomeriggio
In the evening	Di sera
Here/there	Qui/Là
Good/bad	Buono/Cattivo
Big/small	Grande/Piccolo
Cheap/expensive	Economico/Caro
Hot/cold	Caldo/Freddo
Near/far	Vicino/Lontano
Vacant/occupied	Libero/Occupato
With/without	Con/Senza
More/less	Più/Meno
Enough, no more	Basta
Mr...	Signor...
Mrs...	Signora...
Miss...	Signorina... (il Signor, la Signora, la Signorina when speaking about someone else)

SOME SIGNS

Entrance/exit	Entrata/Uscita
Open/closed	Aperto/Chiuso
Arrivals/departures	Arrivi/Partenze
Closed for restoration	Chiuso per restauro
Closed for holidays	Chiuso per ferie
Pull/push	Tirare/Spingere
Beware	Attenzione
No smoking	Vietato fumare

NUMBERS

1	uno
2	due
3	tre
4	quattro
5	cinque
6	sei
7	sette
8	otto
9	nove
10	dieci
11	undici
12	dodici
13	tredici
14	quattordici
15	quindici
16	sedici
17	diciassette
18	diciotto
19	diciannove
20	venti
21	ventuno
22	ventidue
30	trenta
40	quaranta
50	cinquanta
60	sessanta
70	settanta
80	ottanta
90	novanta
100	cento
101	centuno
110	centodieci
200	duecento
500	cinquecento
1000	mille
5000	cinquemila

TRANSPORT

Ferry	Traghetto
Bus station	Autostazione
Train station	Stazione ferroviaria
A ticket to...	Un biglietto a...
One-way/return	Solo andata/andata e ritorno
What time does it leave?	A che ora parte?
Where does it leave from?	Da dove parte?

ACCOMMODATION

Hotel	Albergo
Do you have a room...for one/ two/three people for one/two nights with a double bed?	Ha una cámera... per una/due/ tre person(a/e) per una/due nott(e/i) con un letto matrimoniale?
shower/bath	doccia/bagno
Is breakfast included?	È compresa la prima colazione?
I'll take it	La prendo
I have a booking	Ho una prenotazione
Youth hostel	Ostello per la gioventù

IN THE RESTAURANT

A table	Una tavola
I'd like to book a table for two people at 8pm	Vorrei prenotare una tavola per due alle otto
We need a knife	Abbiamo bisogno di un coltello
a fork	una forchetta
a spoon	un cucchiaio
a glass	un bicchiere
What do you recommend?	Che cosa mi consiglia lei?
Waiter/waitress!	Cameriere/a!
Bill/check	Il conto
Is service included	È incluso il servizio?
I'm a vegetarian	Sono vegetariano/a

QUESTIONS AND DIRECTIONS

Where?	Dove?
Where is/are...?	Dov'è/Dove sono?
When?	Quando?
What? (What is it?)	Cosa? (Cos'è?)
How much/many?	Quanto/Quanti?
Why?	Perché?
It is/There is (is it/is there...?)	È/C'è (È/C'è...?)
What time is it?	Che ora è/Che ore sono?
How do I get to...?	Come arrivo a...?
What time does it open/close?	A che ora apre/chiude?
How much does it/they cost?	Quanto costa/cóstano?

Menu reader
BASICS AND SNACKS

Aceto	Vinegar
Aglio	Garlic
Biscotti	Biscuits
Burro	Butter
Cioccolato	Chocolate
Formaggio	Cheese
Frittata	Omelette
Grissini	Bread sticks
Marmellata	Jam
Olio	Oil
Olive	Olives
Pane	Bread
Pane integrale	Wholemeal bread
Panino	Bread roll
Patatine	Crisps
Patatine fritte	Chips
Pepe	Pepper
Pizzetta	Small cheese-and-tomato pizza
Riso	Rice
Sale	Salt
Tramezzini	Sandwich
Uova	Eggs
Yogurt	Yoghurt
Zúcchero	Sugar
Zuppa	Soup

STARTERS (ANTIPASTI)

Antipasto misto	Mixed cold meats and cheese (and other starters)
Caponata	Mixed aubergine, olives, tomatoes and celery
Caprese	Tomato and mozzarella salad
Insalata di mare	Seafood salad
Insalata di riso	Rice salad
Melanzane in parmigiana	Fried aubergine in tomato and parmesan cheese
Mortadella	Salami-type cured meat
Pancetta	Bacon
Peperonata	Grilled peppers stewed in olive oil
Pomodori ripieni	Stuffed tomatoes
Prosciutto	Ham
Salame	Salami

SOUPS

Brodo	Clear broth
Minestrina	Any light soup
Minestrone	Thick vegetable soup
Pasta e fagioli	Pasta soup with beans
Pastina in brodo	Pasta pieces in clear broth
Stracciatella	Broth with egg

PASTA SAUCES

Aglio e olio (e peperoncino)	Garlic and olive oil (and hot chillies)
Arrabbiata	Spicy tomato sauce
Bolognese	Meat sauce
Burro e salvia	Butter and sage
Carbonara	Cream, ham and beaten egg
Frutta di mare	Seafood
Funghi	Mushroom
Matriciana	Pork and tomato
Panna	Cream
Parmigiano	Parmesan cheese
Pesto	Basil, pine nut, garlic and pecorino sauce
Pomodoro	Tomato sauce
Ragù	Meat sauce
Vóngole	Clam and tomato

MEAT (CARNE)

Agnello	Lamb
Bistecca	Steak
Coniglio	Rabbit
Costolette	Chops
Cotolette	Cutlets
Fegatini	Chicken livers
Fégato	Liver
Involtini	Steak slices, rolled and stuffed
Lingua	Tongue
Maiale	Pork
Manzo	Beef
Ossobuco	Shin of veal
Pollo	Chicken

Polpette	Meatballs
Rognoni	Kidneys
Salsiccia	Sausage
Saltimbocca	Veal with ham
Spezzatino	Stew
Tacchino	Turkey
Trippa	Tripe
Vitello	Veal

FISH (PESCE) AND SHELLFISH (CROSTACEI)

Acciughe	Anchovies
Anguilla	Eel
Aragosta	Lobster
Baccalà	Dried salted cod
Bronzino/Branzino	Sea-bass
Calamari	Squid
Cape lungue	Razor clams
Cape sante	Scallops
Caparossoli	Shrimps
Coda di rospo	Monkfish
Cozze	Mussels
Dentice	Dentex (like sea-bass)
Gamberetti	Shrimps
Gámberi	Prawns
Granchio	Crab
Merluzzo	Cod
Orata	Bream
Ostriche	Oysters
Pescespada	Swordfish
Pólipo	Octopus
Ricci di mare	Sea urchins
Rombo	Turbot
San Pietro	John Dory
Sarde	Sardines
Schie	Shrimps
Seppie	Cuttlefish
Sógliola	Sole
Tonno	Tuna
Triglie	Red mullet
Trota	Trout
Vóngole	Clams

VEGETABLES (CONTORNI) AND SALAD (INSALATA)

Asparagi	Asparagus
Basílico	Basil
Bróccoli	Broccoli
Cápperi	Capers
Carciofi	Artichokes
Carciofini	Artichoke hearts
Carotte	Carrots
Cavolfiori	Cauliflower
Cávolo	Cabbage
Ceci	Chickpeas
Cetriolo	Cucumber
Cipolla	Onion
Fagioli	Beans
Fagiolini	Green beans
Finocchio	Fennel
Funghi	Mushrooms
Insalata verde/ insalata mista	Green salad/mixed salad
Melanzana	Aubergine/eggplant
Orígano	Oregano
Patate	Potatoes
Peperoni	Peppers
Piselli	Peas
Pomodori	Tomatoes
Radicchio	Chicory
Spinaci	Spinach
Zucca	Pumpkin
Zucchini	Courgettes

DESSERTS (DOLCI)

Cassata	Ice-cream cake with candied fruit
Gelato	Ice cream
Macedonia	Fruit salad
Torta	Cake, tart
Zabaglione	Dessert made with eggs, sugar and Marsala wine
Zuppa Inglese	Trifle

FRUIT (FRUTTA) AND NUTS (NOCE)

Ananas	Pineapple
Anguria/Coccómero	Watermelon
Arance Banane	Bananas
Ciliegie	Cherries
Fichi	Figs
Fichi d'India	Prickly pears
Frágole	Strawberries
Limone	Lemon
Mándorle	Almonds
Mele	Apples
Melone	Melon

Pere	Pears
Pesche	Peaches
Pignoli	Pine nuts
Uva	Grapes

DRINKS (BEVANDE)

Acqua minerale	Mineral water
Aranciata	Orangeade
Bicchiere	Glass
Birra	Beer
Bottiglia	Bottle
Caffè	Coffee
Cioccolata calda	Hot chocolate
Ghiaccio	Ice
Granita	Iced coffee or fruit drink
Latte	Milk
Limonata	Lemonade
Selz	Soda water
Spremuta	Fresh fruit juice
Spumante	Sparkling wine
Succo	Fruit juice with sugar
Tò	Tea
Tónico	Tonic water
Vino	Wine
Rosso	Red
Bianco	White
Rosato	Rosé
Secco	Dry
Dolce	Sweet
Litro	Litre
Mezzo	Half
Quarto	Quarter
Salute!	Cheers!

Venetian specialities
ANTIPASTI E PRIMI (FIRST COURSE)

Acciughe marinate	Marinated anchovies with onions
Bigoli in salsa	Spaghetti with butter, onions and sardines
Brodetto	Mixed fish soup, often with tomatoes and garlic
Castraura	Artichoke hearts
Granseola alla Veneziana	Crab cooked with oil, parsley and lemon
Pasta e fagioli	Pasta and beans
Prosciutto San Daniele	The best-quality prosciutto
Risotto alla sbirraglia	Risotto with chicken, ham and vegetables
Risotto alla trevigiana	Butter, onions and chicory risotto
Risotto di cape	Risotto with clams and shellfish
Risotto di mare	Seafood risotto
Sopa de peoci	Mussel soup with garlic and parsley

SECONDI (SECOND COURSE)

Anguilla alla Veneziana	Eel cooked with lemon and tuna
Baccalà mantecato	Salt cod simmered in milk
Fegato veneziana	Sliced calf's liver cooked in olive oil with onion
Peoci salati	Mussels with parsley and garlic
Risi e bisi	Rice and peas, with parmesan and ham
Sarde in saor	Marinated sardines
Seppie in nero	Squid cooked in its ink
Seppioline nere	Baby cuttlefish cooked in its ink

DOLCI (DESSERTS)

Frittole alla Veneziana	Rum and anise flavoured fritters filled with pine nuts, raisins and candied fruit
Tiramisù	Layered dessert of savoiardi biscuits dipped in coffee and/or rum, and a mixture of mascarpone, egg yolks and sugar, dusted with cocoa

PUBLISHING INFORMATION

This third edition published February 2016 by **Rough Guides Ltd**.
80 Strand, London WC2R 0RL
11, Community Centre, Panchsheel Park, New Delhi 110017, India
Distributed by Penguin Random House
Penguin Books Ltd, 80 Strand, London WC2R 0RL
Penguin Group (USA) 345 Hudson Street, NY 10014, USA
Penguin Group (Australia) 250 Camberwell Road, Camberwell, Victoria 3124, Australia
Penguin Group (NZ) 67 Apollo Drive, Mairangi Bay, Auckland 1310, New Zealand
Penguin Group (South Africa) Block D, Rosebank Office Park, 181 Jan Smuts Avenue,
Parktown North, Gauteng, South Africa 2193
Rough Guides is represented in Canada by
Tourmaline Editions Inc. 662 King Street West, Suite 304,Toronto, Ontario M5V 1M7
Typeset in Minion and Din to an original design by Henry Iles and Dan May.
Printed and bound in Malaysia by Vivar Printing Sdn. Bhd.
© Jonathan Buckley 2016
Maps © Rough Guides

176pp includes index
A catalogue record for this book is available from the British Library
ISBN 978-0-24120-428-3

The publishers and authors have done their best to ensure the accuracy and currency of all the
information in the **Pocket Rough Guide Venice**, however, they can accept no responsibility for
any loss, injury, or inconvenience sustained by any traveller as a result of information or advice
contained in the guide.
1 3 5 7 9 8 6 4 2

ROUGH GUIDES CREDITS

Editor: Olivia Rawes
Layout: Pradeep Thapliyal
Cartography: Katie Bennett
Picture editor: Phoebe Lowndes
Photographers: Michelle Grant, James McCon-
nachie and Martin Richardson
Proofreader: Susannah Wight

Managing editor: Monica Woods
Production: Jimmy Lao
Cover design: Nicole Newman
Editorial assistant: Freya Godfrey
Senior pre-press designer: Dan May
Publisher: Keith Drew
Publishing director: Georgina Dee

THE AUTHOR

Jonathan Buckley has written and contributed to several Rough Guides on Italy and music. He has
also published nine novels, and was shortlisted for the 2015 BBC National Short Story Award. He
lives in Brighton.

ACKNOWLEDGEMENTS

Jonathan Buckley Many thanks to Olivia Rawes for speedy and painless editing.

HELP US UPDATE

We've gone to a lot of effort to ensure that the third edition of the **Pocket Rough Guide Venice** is accurate and up-to-date. However, things change – places get "discovered", opening hours are notoriously fickle, restaurants and rooms raise prices or lower standards. If you feel we've got it wrong or left something out, we'd like to know, and if you can remember the address, the price, the hours, the phone number, so much the better.

Please send your comments with the subject line "**Pocket Rough Guide Venice Update**" to mail@roughguides.com. We'll credit all contributions and send a copy of the next edition (or any other Rough Guide if you prefer) for the very best emails.

Find travel information, connect with fellow travellers and book your trip on Ⓦ roughguides.com

READERS' UPDATES

Thanks to all the readers who have taken the time to write in with comments and suggestions (and apologies if we've inadvertently omitted or misspelt anyone's name):

Alessandra Curci, Nick Evans, Dennis Jackson, Margot O'Keeffe, David Parish and Sue Wall

PHOTO CREDITS

All photos ⒸⒸ Rough Guides except the following:
(Key: t-top; c-centre; b-bottom; l-left; r-right)

Index

Maps are marked in **bold**.

T

V

W

Z